AT THE
FIELD'S EDGE
ADRIAN BELL AND THE
ENGLISH COUNTRYSIDE

For

Bob and Elizabeth Rose Hawking

AT THE
FIELD'S EDGE
ADRIAN BELL AND THE
ENGLISH COUNTRYSIDE

Richard Hawking

ROBERT HALE

First published in 2019 by
Robert Hale, an imprint of
The Crowood Press Ltd,
Ramsbury, Marlborough
Wiltshire SN8 2HR

www.crowood.com

British Library Cataloguing-in-Publication Data
A catalogue record for this book is available from the
British Library.

ISBN 978 0 7198 2906 2

All artwork by Harry Becker

Typeset by Chapter One Book Production, Knebworth

Printed and bound in India by Parksons Graphics

❧ CONTENTS ❧

❧ FOREWORD ❧

I AM, PERHAPS, AN UNLIKELY person to write the foreword of this book. I have no significant literary or academic achievements to my name, and before Richard approached me with his draft of the book you're about to read, I was entirely ignorant of the work of Adrian Bell. I am, though, a second generation farmer on one of the few small mixed family farms left in Britain. We grow vegetables, run sheep through our pastures, harvest apples from our orchards, and coppice firewood from our copse and hedgerows. As you can imagine, I never thought I would be writing a foreword for a literary work, but as I read *At the Field's Edge* I found in Bell's work a voice that articulated so many of my own experiences and reflections that I thought perhaps I may have something of value to add as someone attempting to live and work the land in a way in which, I hope, Bell would have approved of.

The past century has seen the most extensive and extreme transformation of agriculture since the first handful of grasses and wild animals were domesticated to our service some 12,000 years ago. The use of petrochemicals, heavy machinery and more subtle technologies such as genome editing have allowed us to push back against the boundaries that ecosystems had enforced upon farmers for millennia. Fuelled by a period of unprecedented economic growth, and the centralization of markets by corporations, the past century has seen the great majority of small, diverse farms fall by the wayside to make way for the new breed of subsidized industrial megafarms capable of producing enormous quantities of product for the commodity markets. Bell was there at the birth of industrial agriculture in Britain and saw it grow through its infancy

6

into its coming of age as the meadows and mixed grain and vegetable farms – which had fed the population of Britain for countless generations – were ploughed in and consolidated into vast monocultures. Bell saw that these 'advances' set a dangerous and precarious precedent for future generations and instinctively understood that these practices were undermining the ecological processes that make all life on earth possible.

However, it's not Bell's logic that has stuck with me most forcefully, but it is his deep, poetic and heartfelt reflections of living in the British countryside. For we are lucky in the extreme to have been gifted a land of such stunning beauty and rich abundance. In my travels across various continents, I have never found a land that feels remotely as soft and generous as the British countryside. It is remarkable that, even in the face of such rampant industrialization, we retain so much of the character imbued into the landscape by the lives of innumerable landworkers. There is, though, a danger of looking at pre-industrial agriculture through the rose-tinted glasses of nostalgia, and it's very important to realise that industrial agriculture has often only exacerbated pre-existing problems in agricultural practices. Many of the world's soils and habitats had already been severely degraded by tillage and overgrazing long before the rumble of tractors was ever heard in the fields.

We are undoubtedly on the cusp of yet another revolution in agriculture. Farmers the world over are seeing through the supposed silver bullets presented by agritech and agrochemical companies, and finding solutions within ecosystems. Graziers are bringing health and diversity back to the world's pastures and grasslands by mimicking the predator/prey relationships that drive grassland fertility. Growers and arable farmers are using new understandings of soil biology to reduce tillage and holistically improve soil fertility without the use of synthetic chemicals. Farmers of all disciplines are finding innovative ways of reintroducing trees into our agricultural landscapes. Building on the legacies of visionaries like Bell, this new breed of farmers are combining new technologies and the latest scientific insights with time-honoured farming practices to create solutions which work for them whilst simultaneously sequestering atmospheric carbon and providing vital habitat for wildlife. It's here at the field's edge, where worlds meet, we find life at its most vibrant and elemental.

Jake Eldridge
Oxton Organics,
Worcestershire,
December 2018

❦ ACKNOWLEDGEMENTS ❦

FIRSTLY I WOULD LIKE to thank John Ford, the President of the Adrian Bell Society, for his wonderful commitment to keeping the writing of Bell alive, and for supporting me in my own interests in Adrian Bell. The work that John and his colleagues have done over the years to ensure that the Adrian Bell Society continues to promote and share their love of Bell's writing should not be underestimated.

I would also like to offer my gratitude to Ann Gander, whose biography of Adrian Bell – *Adrian Bell: The Voice of the Countryside* – proved to be an invaluable resource. I am much indebted to all her research and writing, which I have used for the benefit of this book. My thanks also to Adrian's grandson, Richard Kamm, and to Rosemary Dixon of the *Eastern Daily Press* who kindly provided the photographs within, as well as to The Crowood Press. Thanks also to Nicholas Holloway, and to the owners of the Harry Becker pictures for their support in allowing his paintings to once again complement the work of Adrian Bell.

My sincere appreciation to the Bell Family, especially Adrian's children Martin, Anthea and Sylvia, for allowing me access to Adrian Bell's notebooks and archives, and for the openness with which they have regarded my proposal for *At the Field's Edge*. I sincerely hope that in this exploration I have done some justice to your father's wonderful writing. And thank you to Alexander Stilwell for his foresight, perseverance and patience as commissioning editor. His belief and support for this book, together with his own interest in Adrian Bell's writing, has been invaluable.

On a personal note, thank you to Mal, Phil, Ang, Wayne, Maria,

Andrew, Jane, Sarah, Will, Dan, Kirsty and Elisa for their continued interest and encouragement during the writing of this book – it has been very much appreciated. Particular thanks to Rich and James for setting, in their own inimitable ways, examples of what can be achieved through commitment, passion and humour – your belief and support kept me going on cold, grey winter Sundays. And to Simon and Paul, for sharing with me what seems, as time passes, an idyllic childhood. We really were very lucky.

Finally, I would like to thank Melanie. Not only has she spent hours and hours editing, and trying to tease out very well hidden arguments, she also had to endure even more time listening to, and counselling me through my various writing traumas/tantrums. As no doubt most of our friends would readily and wholeheartedly agree, this book would never have been written without her. And unlike the chicken debate, they would be right.

❧ PREFACE ❧

MY OWN INTEREST IN farming, rural communities and the countryside stems from my experiences growing up on a small farm in Somerset in the 1970s and 1980s. My father and his father's farming overlapped Adrian Bell's years as a farmer from the 1920s to Bell's death in 1980. With my father's death in 1998, the agriculture tenancy held for generations by our family came to an end.

At the time of his death I was in my mid-twenties, away at university and without a care in the world. Within two weeks I was scattering the local soil that he once tilled on to his coffin. Within six months the farm was being auctioned. It was early spring, but the cold, misty morning suggested winter. Reluctant cattle were herded from straw-filled sheds into the cold, open pens, and farm machinery from a dark barn was moved on to a damp yard into the vaporous light of morning. For many of the older implements, it was the first time they had seen the light of day for many years. The collection of old and not so old looked rather pathetic when laid out in that way. Removed from a proper context their functionality was lost, and their meaning and past worth dissolved: they were relics of a time past. Having had to deal with my father's personal belongings, my mother chose to remain indoors throughout the sale, and saw the artefacts of a dedicated farming life pass by her window and away forever.

I was beginning to appreciate that the agricultural tradition that he had spent his life following was dying with him. My mother continued to live in the farmhouse until she died five years ago. The farm buildings and the paddocks surrounding it had long since been sold by the council, and are now an expensive retirement village.

It was shortly after her death, after my brothers and I had finally cleared the farmhouse of at least three generations of belongings, that I first encountered the writing of Adrian Bell – as a farmer's son, the evocative title *Men and the Fields* drew me immediately to it. I rarely spoke at any length to my father about his life farming as a young man. However, upon reading *Men and the Fields* – twenty years after my father's death – I finally got a sense of the nature of the stories that he may have told me. Like Adrian Bell, my father and grandfather ran small mixed farms, and, like Bell, struggled to see the long-term wisdom of the changes in agricultural practice in the mid-twentieth century.

Thus, the inspiration behind *At the Field's Edge* stems from both Bell's wonderful writing, together with the observations made, and the knowledge that was shared, within rural communities such as the one in which I grew up. One of my most evocative memories is standing at a field's edge listening to my father talk about the countryside with others who had a deep respect and appreciation not only of its practicality, but also of its beauty. His eyes would roam the familiar green landscape where he truly lived, and where I really got to know him. Bell shares this view, and renders it with sensitivity across fifty years, a time when the English countryside was controlled and changed more than ever before. It is a view that we all need to pay attention to if we are to address some of these changes and reconnect not only to our environment, but also to each other.

❧ INTRODUCTION: AT THE FIELD'S EDGE ❧

PAUSING 'AT THE FIELD'S EDGE' is a purposeful habit of farmers. It is their opportunity to survey the field and assess its future uses and needs. At the same time, it is also a reflective moment when farmers contemplate their own relationship with, and appreciation for, the land. *At the Field's Edge* hopes to take such a practical as well as reflective and appreciative approach. The book pauses to offer the reader unfamiliar with Adrian Bell an introduction to the prose and ideas of this important writer. At the same time, it provides those readers well versed in writers of the countryside with a thoughtful and engaging exploration of Bell's writing, and his 'practical' relevance to contemporary debates about the countryside. In doing so, it will address factors that continue to impact and jeopardize our countryside: the rise of industrial farming and its environmental impact on the countryside; the growing separation of the country and the city; and the disconnection of producer and consumer, and the impact of capitalist consumerism on the countryside. In these considerations, *At the Field's Edge* will also examine how these factors have contributed to the decline of rural communities and rural culture, and how they challenge constructions of English identity.

Adrian Bell is the perfect writer to help a largely urban population reconnect with England's land and the values enshrined in farming life. Born in 1901 in London, Adrian Bell came from an educated, middle-class family and was destined for a career in the city. However, he became disillusioned with his options very quickly, and made the radical decision to become an apprentice farmer, moving to Suffolk in 1920. He wrote his first book, *Corduroy*, in 1929, and although there

Suffolk Sky

were periods of time during the next fifty years when he stopped farming, he continued to write about rural life until his death in 1980. In total he published twenty-five books, most of which were based on his life and work in Suffolk; he also contributed many articles to various magazines and anthologies throughout his life; and from 1950 to 1980 his *Countryman's Notebook* was a weekly feature in the *Eastern Daily Press*, published in Suffolk. In 1930 he also set the first *Times* crossword – the first to appear in any publication in Britain – and went on to compile over four thousand in a fifty-year period. Bell understood farming and rural life, but he was, first and foremost, an indefatigable and engaging writer.

Throughout his writing Bell frames and enhances our view of the countryside. If we pause at the field's edge with him for a moment and reflect on, for example, the wild rose, we get a lesson not only in aesthetic appreciation, but also a message about what is disappearing from the countryside. In *Apple Acre* (1940), he describes the wild roses that could be found around the edges of his fields. He implies the importance of the relationship between the 'practical' field and its wider environment when he writes:

The long days blow the wild roses. They open and are soon bleached white. The buds at the first show are even crimson: points of crimson. Opening cup-shaped, with still the crumple in their petals, they are at their true colour, a flush so delicate you cannot tell where it begins and ends, with the thick saffron ring of pollen round the centres. These differing colours harmonizing because there is life shining out of them, and not merely colours. […] The roses open and bleach and reflect back the light. They focus the beams like lenses; to look at them long is dazzling. By noon the whole bush is flashing with white, wide-open roses. It is their final shape, that of a Maltese cross with one too many arms. A white butterfly comes over the hedge, followed by another. But at another glance I see they are two petals: they have already begun to fall.

Celebrating nature's 'harmonizing' beauty, yet lamenting her inevitable decay and the 'fall', this is a writer who looks with honest eyes at the changes he sees happening around him.

While Bell constantly assessed and described the diurnal changes that he noticed in the countryside about him, he also sought to educate his readers about the larger and long-term picture. Thus in the same work he also notes how:

> The concern for the home-grown and the home-made was one of the conditions which gave a tone of emergency to the writing of this book. [...] Our emphasis was on organic farming and living. We felt that a balanced life of people in an organic relationship with their home place was important. Compost, of course, was a potent word among us; the utilisation of natural wastes. The basic premise of the Kinship in Husbandry was that man was plundering the earth's resources at a spendthrift rate and impoverishing posterity. [...] Today, food production is becoming more like a branch of big business year by year. (*Apple Acre*, 1940)

Bell's Kinship in Husbandry evolved into today's Soil Association, and the concerns he expresses above are even more pressing in the twenty-first century. *At the Field's Edge* shows how Bell was living and writing on the eve of, and during, an agricultural revolution himself, and therefore felt the same urgency as many of us do today. Using his concerns as a focusing lens, this book considers the changing agricultural practices he witnessed, and their effect on our countryside. For example, increasing mechanization, together with the hugely significant 1947 Agriculture Act, which enshrined the subsidy system, led to the decline of small farms and the beginning of agribusinesses. Monoculture and industrialization has transformed not only the look, but the ecology and economy of the land Bell once lived and worked on.

Indeed, in the fifty years since the Agriculture Act, which pushed subsidies for farmers and encouraged production through increasing industrialization of farming, more than 150,000 miles of hedgerows have been lost, flower-rich meadowland has declined by 97 per cent, and the diversity of wildlife – from tree sparrows and corn buntings to butterflies and hedgehogs – has been decimated. But it is not just the environment that has been affected: it has also impacted on those who work and live in rural communities. Bell foresaw the possible effects of this 'progress'. Consequently, this book tries to show that Bell's values and vision of husbandry should inform our own relationship with, and future custody of, the countryside.

There are signs that the traditional methods of husbandry advocated by Bell are beginning once again to gain traction. The Campaign to Protect Rural England's recent publication *2026 Vision for the Countryside* notes that 'the role of farming in helping to deliver a brighter, better future is critical. This vision sets out our aspirations for a farming system which, by 2026, will be helping to create a more vibrant countryside, environ- mentally, socially and economically.' Moreover, greater numbers of people have become interested in environmental concerns at a more local level in recent years. An effect of this is a desire from consumers to re- establish a stronger relationship with the countryside. For example, there is a growing availability and popularity of organic produce through box schemes and farm shops, whilst two primarily locally sourced 'organic' motorway service stations now exist off the M6 and M5 motorways. You can now buy 'wonky vegetables' in supermarkets, with some offering 'Wonky Selection Boxes'. Moreover, in an article in *The Guardian* in 2012 entitled 'London 2012: How Rural Writing Inspired the Olympic Opening Ceremony', Jamie Andrews highlights that this 'greening' of the public conscience influenced the vision of Britain that was presented to billions around the world. Indications of a growing political base are also evident, with, for example, Green Party membership doubling in recent years.

This greening of the public conscience has in part been inspired by an expanding readership for literature about the countryside, with a growing range of publications that explore our relationship with the immediate natural world. Writers such as Robert Macfarlane, Roger Deakin, W. G. Sebald, Jonathan Bate, Tim Dee, Richard Mabey, Madeleine Bunting and Chris Yates follow in the tradition of earlier authors writing about farming and the countryside, including Richard Jefferies, Edward Thomas, H. J. Massingham, W. H. Hudson, John Stewart Collis and Ronald Blythe. Nature writing, often synonymous with rural literature or countryside writing, has finally developed a wider appeal and reader-ship, so that every bookshop has its countryside shelf or, increasingly, its 'nature table'. Happily it appears that Bell, too, is enjoying a resurgence of interest. This is evident in the republications of *Corduroy* (2009), *Silver Ley* (2015) and *The Cherry Tree* (2017) by Slightly Foxed, and *Men and the Fields* (2009) and *Apple Acre* (2012) by Little Toller. Naturally I highly recommend that you pick up some copies.

In his wonderful book *Landscape and Englishness*, David Matless exemplifies the nature-writing trend, noting that there has been a 'cultural braiding of the Green' in the twenty-first century. He cites the popularity of *Midsomer Murders* (1997 to the present day) and Jez Butterworth's play *Jerusalem* (2009), in addition to the opening cere-mony of the London Olympics in 2012 to illustrate how the rural appears to be reflected more significantly in popular culture. He also argues that contemporary and historical constructions of Englishness, and thus English identity, are largely associated with the country, not the city. For example, Matless notes how Paul Fussell and others have argued that 'many formulations of national identity in the 1914–18 war were based on constructions of Englishness built on visions of rural – not urban – England'. Indeed, Stanley Baldwin – Conservative Prime Minister from 1924–29 and 1935–37, and hugely influential in government in the intervening years – viewed England very much in pastoral terms: 'To me, England is country, and the country is England. And when I ask myself what I mean by England … England comes to me through my various senses.' Matless observes that, for Baldwin, England was comprised of 'corncrakes and scythes, the sight of a plough-team, the smell of wood smoke'. Baldwin's vision of Englishness – and thus national identity – remains a persuasive one in the twenty-first century.

It is unsurprising, given how the English countryside is often syn-onymous with Englishness, that rural literature continues to be a popular topic with a wide readership. Matless notes that it has, in fact, become a minor publishing phenomenon: 'If Englishness has offered publishers a niche theme for the twenty-first century, nature has become a richer seam.' Despite the variety of styles and voices of such publications, common to all of them is that nature is conflated with culture and, ultimately, identity politics. As Matless argues: 'The power of landscape resides in it being simultaneously a site of economic, social, political and aesthetic value', and a 'vehicle of social and self-identity, as a site for the claiming of a cultural authority, as a generator of profit, as a space for different types of living'. In other words, the English countryside informs and shapes each and every one of us.

In this context, Adrian Bell's work is at the nexus of current trends in environmental literature, and he deserves wider recognition. Therefore, *At the Field's Edge* offers an in-depth appreciation of Adrian Bell's writing, and seeks to deepen and extend the discussion of modern writers of environmental literature. However, many of these writers offer very personal meditations, or express imaginative biographical interpretations of specific places. They increasingly blur the lines between non-fiction genres such as biography, environmental literature, ecocriticism, history, travel and memoir. Steven Poole, reflecting rather negatively on the growing popularity of nature writing in *The Guardian* in 2013, referred to the trend as a 'solidly bourgeois form of escapism'.

As the following chapters document, Bell is not about such escapism, and reading him is not simply about indulging in a nostalgic vision of a once great but now declining countryside. Bell understood the toil inherent in his relationship with the countryside; his view of it is not an aesthetic one. Although he did appreciate its beauty, he also understood, and aimed to portray in his writing, the value gained in our interaction with the countryside. By exploring Bell's account of his years of practical experience as a farmer, this book emphasizes the interdependence of producers and consumers, and the impact their growing separation has had, and continues to have, on our countryside.

Likewise, Bell's writing has a truthfulness borne out of his years working with the land, and he combines that candour with an equally open appreciation and connection with the rural communities he knew all his life, and from which he rarely strayed. He fundamentally understood the land and human nature, and saw and predicted the many problems we have created in our unthinking interactions with the countryside. As such, the contemporary relevance of his ideas, together with the clarity of his poetic prose, will appeal to readers not only of 'nature writing', but also to readers with more environmental, social and political concerns. Bell's writings and ideas have a fundamental relevance to our embedded relationship with our natural environment. A reader of his work begins to appreciate that the values integral to the life he depicts were truer, and its rewards deeper, than anything that economic progress can give us. Indeed, Bell's 'old ways' – non-intensive, mixed method farming – have significant relevance to our evolving stewardship of the countryside today.

Therefore, Bell's insightful observations during a time of huge changes in farming methods deserve to be re-evaluated: he reflects directly and frequently on the environmental, social and economic impact he sees around him, and fears for the future of communities and the countryside. Consequently, this study is the first to situate and assess Bell's writing in relation to the significant influences the British countryside was subject to during the mid-twentieth century. Bell witnessed at first hand these changes: rapid mechanization, intensification, and the introduction and widespread use of artificial fertilizers and pesticides. He also foresaw the impact that such changes – the decline of hedgerows, increasing monoculture, the growing separation between the producer and the consumer – would have on the English countryside and our relationship to it.

With such developments in mind, the book is structured around the fundamental theme of Adrian Bell's work: that of change and its impact on the countryside. Throughout his writing, he observes the change around him, and comments upon the consequences of the technological and scientific developments he sees. At the heart of each chapter are Bell's observations and reflections on the countryside. These are taken from a wide selection of his non-fiction works, and arranged chronologically in order to map the changing countryside and his response to these changes. Each chapter broadens this appreciation by discussing the contemporary relevance of his views. In doing so, the book explores the relationship between his writing and the past and present environmental, social and economic challenges faced by the countryside. Each chapter presents Bell's vision of an organic, sustainable and diverse method of farming in which we do not exploit our environment, but instead endeavour to work in harmony with it.

George Henderson in his best-selling book *The Farming Ladder* (1943), maintained that there was only one rule of good husbandry: 'To leave the land in better heart than it was found.' With this in mind, I shall discuss how we have fallen far short of this guiding principle. However, by exploring Bell's relevant views on farming methods, this book presents to the reader ways in which we can recover such a practical and vital vision for our countryside. Pausing at the field's edge with Bell will hopefully encourage readers, farmers, consumers, and maybe even policy makers, to take a moment to consider the future of the field, and the many interconnected fields and lives that make up the British countryside. His voice, although currently a largely unfamiliar one, has vitally important things to say to all of us about the future of the English countryside.

Horse and Cart

❧ 1 ❧

RURAL ENGLAND AND AGRICULTURAL CHANGE

To UNDERSTAND AND APPRECIATE Bell's place in agricultural history and rural writing, it helps to know a little about the politicization of farming in Britain in the last 200 years. For those who know this history, you may want to skim or skip over the ensuing chapter. This chapter is about historicizing and synthesizing the range of factors that impacted on farming in the last century. It also aims to introduce and/or remind readers of the wealth of important and influential writers and writings about our rural heritage. For example, for those readers who have never encountered the great voices of the past such as H. J. Massingham or John Stewart Collis, or their modern counterparts such as Roland Blythe and Richard Mabey, I hope this chapter proves enlightening.

Bell started farming in 1920, but the roots of the industrial revolution of agriculture that he witnessed throughout the twentieth century can be traced back to the early nineteenth, if not eighteenth century. Indeed, as Bell's contemporary, the great writer about farming and rural philosopher H. J. Massingham observed, Bell himself forms a line of descent from the William Cobbett tradition of 'high' farming. Cobbett (1763–1835), author of, amongst other books, *Rural Rides* and *Cottage Economy*, was a great reformer and strong advocate for farming communities, but he was also focused on the health of the land. In *Rural Rides* (1830) Cobbett was prescient enough to raise early warning signs regarding the dangers of specialism, abstraction and generalizing knowledge, believing that these undermined independence. He argued that such centralized state and industry ideologies would teach 'submission to the order existing at the hour, which was becoming increasingly urban and industrial'. Instead, Cobbett valued all-roundedness, self-help, versatility and concrete experience. As a result, he fought for the skilled labour of the craftsman, and for the economic freedom that smallholdings could provide individuals and their immediate communities. He fought, in other words, for individualism and independence. He famously resisted enclosure because he saw that agriculture was in danger of being irrevocably changed as the industrial revolution and an increasingly capitalist economy took hold in Victorian Britain.

Like Cobbett, but writing almost one hundred years later, Massingham was deeply concerned about the direction in which agriculture in England was heading. Massingham therefore pointed to Cobbett's concerns, and argued that such a voice needed to be listened to by a new generation, particularly those who had influence over our countryside. Massingham asserts that 'to heed [Cobbett's] vision of England would be to return to ourselves' – that is, to return to a well managed countryside that supports our sense of individual and collective cultural identity, but also, of course, quite literally supports a healthy population.

As I noted above, Massingham viewed Adrian Bell as a contemporary prophet of the countryside, so it is not surprising to find that Cobbett and Bell share similar philosophies and ideologies in relation to how we should farm the land. For example, both Cobbett and Bell believed in mixed farming. Fundamental to mixed farming is the idea of crop rotation, which not only revitalizes the fertility of the land but also makes it more resistant to pests and disease without the need for chemicals or artificial fertilizers. Such rotation fights infection and helps maintain yields; it also encourages a greater diversity of wildlife in the fields themselves.

Crop rotation has, in fact, taken place since the Middle Ages, because those who work with the land know that it works. Thus when Arthur Young, an eighteenth-century Suffolk farmer, carried out a survey of farming in the Chilterns on behalf of the Board of Agriculture, his reports were full of admiration for the system of crop rotation that he found in Herefordshire. In his report for 1804 he notes that in the first year they sowed turnips, in the second year barley, in the third clover, in the fourth oats, and the fifth wheat. The method of 'folding' – moving animals from one area of a field to another in order to fertilize the soil – was also used to ensure soil quality and consistently good yields. In his recent book, *Grass-Fed Nation* (2016), Graham Harvey, a food and farming journalist and agricultural adviser to the radio programme *The Archers*, reminds us that this rotational system produces the best grass-fed meat, grass-fed milk, butter and cheese, and pasture-raised poultry and eggs, all of which are 'near perfect foods for human nutrition'. Science is proving that some old ways are indeed the best.

However, as the industrial revolution gathered pace in the mid-nineteenth century, greater numbers of people moved away from the countryside to find work in the cities. As a consequence, cheap labour on farms declined, and with it the care of the land. By the start of World War I, the four- or five-year crop rotation that had been practised since the Middle Ages had declined massively. In its place was a simple crop rotation of grain and fallow (that is, ploughed but not sown). During this time, many farmers struggled to diversify their farming because they were too reliant on receiving a stable price for corn. As a result, the good practices observed by Young in 1804, praised by Cobbett in the nineteenth century, and still partially practised by farmers such as Bell in the twentieth century, went into sharp decline.

In 'Farming is the Feet of the Nation' – L. F. Easterbrook's contribution to Massingham's *The Natural Order* (1945), a book to which Bell also contributed, and which will be considered in more detail later – he exemplifies a further decline in agriculture between World Wars I and II: 'A quarter of a million men fled the land. Farm houses, cottages and buildings fell down and, like the neglected fields, became buried under the weedy vegetation.' He adds that this was compounded by the great depression of the early 1930s. Farming was in an increasingly unhealthy condition, but so too was the nation's health. In the 1947 article 'Agriculture and Planning', L. D. Stamp, an economic geographer, noted that before World War II, 30 per cent of the population suffered from preventable malnutritional diseases. As a result, the government decided that there needed to be a greater focus on the production and marketing of staple foods such as milk, eggs and meat, which would not only improve the state of farming, but also the health of the population as a whole.

In order to address these interlinked concerns, a raft of agricultural legislation and policy was introduced throughout the 1930s, with one of the earliest and most significant being the Import Duties Act of 1932. This Act established preferential rates for products culled from the British Empire. In addition to this, the depression had demonstrated a greater need for economic planning, as well as the marketing of agriculture in Britain. A plethora of Acts followed throughout the 1930s with the aim of achieving these twin goals. These included the Wheat Act (1932), the Cattle Industry Act (1934), the Milk Act (1934), the Livestock Industry Act (1937), the Bacon Industry Act (1938) and the Agricultural Development Act (1939).

Two of the most significant Acts in this economic planning and marketing of British agriculture were the Marketing Acts of 1931 and 1933, which sought to regulate the supply and demand of the most common branches of agriculture. They gave powers to the state to control the quantity of both imports and home production. By 1939, Marketing Boards for hops, pigs, milk and potatoes had been set up, giving them the power to buy, sell, grade and store the produce. For example, the Hop Marketing Board had the sole right to sell and fix the scale of prices, and issue basic acreage quotas to every grower. Under the Milk Marketing Scheme, all milk belonged to the Board. These Boards also had the power to impose penalties on farmers for breaches of their regulations.

The impending threat of a second world war intensified and cemented this government intervention in agriculture. As a result, the War Agricultural Committee was set up in 1939 to dramatically increase food production, and had unprecedented powers over farmers and their interaction with the land. These powers included being able to turn out farmers from the land they owned, or had long tenancies on, if they did not comply with the Committee's requests. There was significant resistance amongst some farmers. Quite naturally, they resented being told what they could and couldn't do with the land they had worked for years. C. H. Gardiner, a rural writer and contemporary of Bell, recalls in his 1945 publication *Your Village and Mine*, one farmer's reaction upon being approached by a fellow farmer and the district member of the War Agricultural Committee: 'You won't make me do it,' the local farmer declared. 'Hitler won't make me do it. In fact, God Almighty won't make me plough up that green field.' 'Maybe not', replied the visiting farmer quietly, 'but the War Agricultural Committee will!' In the end, they did do it. By the close of the war, the total output of food had increased by a staggering 70 per cent.

The impetus for national self-sufficiency had numerous positive effects. Easterbrook notes that, 'No sooner did the war compel us to pay farmers fair prices, to give them a semblance of stability and therefore of confidence [... than] there was a resurgence of spirit in the countryside, an uprising of endeavour and enterprise that far exceeded the wildest hopes of the most devoted believer in British agriculture.' The meddling of politicians revitalized agriculture in England and they were quick to claim the credit. In an official statement by the Minister of Agriculture and Fisheries, an article entitled 'Wartime Achievements and Post-War Prospects' published in 1944, the minister, R. S. Hudson, emphasizes the impact the War Agricultural Committee had on farming. He writes how, 'During the war the British farmer has been able to count on an assured market for all he has been able to produce.' However, he continues:

> Is it too much to hope that farmers will respond fully to the guarantee of markets and prices with the certainty that these conditions will prevail for at least another four years? [...] The measure of the farmers' response to this opportunity for sustained high production must have a big influence on the nation's opinion of agriculture as an efficient industry, which can contribute largely to Britain's economy in peace as well as war.

At the same time as he credits the government with establishing a stable market, he questions farmers' commitment to 'sustained high production' (not 'sustainable' it should be noted) and 'efficient industry'. There is no mention of soil or crop health, or indeed of the many farmers, labourers and communities who create and support the 'industry' he speaks of.

At the end of World War II, the National Farmers Union (NFU) understandably lobbied for subsidies to remain in place for the main crops that farmers were now set up to produce. However, these subsidies supported the move away from mixed farms to the development of larger farms. In the drive for self-sufficiency and higher production, more and more pasture land – fundamental to mixed farming – was ploughed up and sown with larger, less diverse crops. This proved to be the first significant step in creating the monoculture that dominates our countryside today. As we shall see, there were numerous voices, including Bell's, who questioned the wisdom of the new, large farm. However, mixed farming was no longer seen as part of the 'efficient industry' so valued by the politicians who were taking credit for increased food production and national self-sufficiency. The 1947 Agricultural Act cemented this vision of efficiency and quantity in policy. Supported by the NFU, Harvey notes that this Act and government subsidies created 'a narrow ideology of intensive farming [that] was accepted almost to the exclusion of all other influences. This ideology maintained food production as the only proper use of land.'

Inevitably, traditional methods of husbandry associated with mixed farming did not receive the support that they needed to survive in this changing agricultural context. Indeed, during the 1950s, *Farmer's Weekly* (the most popular publication for working farmers at the time) increased their praise of the progressive farmers who, fuelled by the subsidies enshrined in the 1947 Agricultural Act for specific large-scale crops, were embracing the modern methods of intensive, mechanized farming. Amongst other financial encouragements there were subsidies for incorporating the use of chemical fertilizers, as well as grants to grub out hedges, uproot old orchards and plough up flower meadows. By the 1960s, subsidies effectively and actively discouraged mixed farming methods.

28

The narrow economic incentive of subsidies, and the broad spread of monocultures, increased as Britain entered the European Union (EU) in 1973. Indeed, EU subsidies further compounded problems. By the 1980s, Graham Harvey notes in his manifesto for mixed farming, *Grass-fed Nation*, that as a result of EU subsidies, 'proper crop rotations were impossible to operate. If you wanted to pick up your subsidy you had to give up real mixed farming.' Richie Tassell, a farmer who grew up in the Northamptonshire countryside, paints a bleak picture of the decline in the 1970s and 1980s in the following statement to Harvey:

> The mixed farms started to go down the pan, and agribusiness began to take over. The farmer next door was one of the last to go, he still had cattle and sheep and arable crops in rotation. A week after he sold up to a big pension fund this fleet of bulldozers arrived. [...] They stripped the hedgerows, the remaining parkland trees, walnut trees two or three hundred years old: the whole lot was gone in a day. [...] The old farmer probably had six full-time staff. You could see them walking across the fields. It all went almost overnight. From then on, everything was done in fleets of big tractors [...] it was like a military operation. [...] That was the worst of times in terms of habitat destruction, almost the final nail in the coffin of what John Clare [the eighteenth-century rural poet] was writing about. He was there at the beginning of the process, I was there at the end. It was a permanent loss. It's all gone.

Many farmers, including my father, could have told similar stories. Indeed, I witnessed such 'bulldozing' procedures when the local council sold off my grandfather's and my father's fields and farms after their deaths. The listed barn was brought down almost overnight, and the fields, trees and hedgerows were levelled, in this case for housing developers rather than monocultures. Writing in 2016, Colin Tudge, a biologist and science writer, states that:

> For arable farming in particular, this past half-century has been conceived as a field exercise in industrial chemistry and heavy engineering,

geared to the maximization of short-term wealth, at least for a few. All the subtlety, and all the respect for the life of the soil, has been overridden.

The industrialization of agriculture, financed by government and latterly EU subsidies, has changed the landscape, the wildlife and the people of the English countryside more significantly than in any previous time that man has farmed the land. Indeed, in his wide-ranging study of who owns and controls the landscape – *Feral* – the economist George Monbiot describes how, after moving from London to rural Wales, he was struck by the absence of wildlife and plant variety that was a consequence of industrial agriculture. He writes: 'The range of flowering plants on the open land was pitiful. Birds of any kind were rare, often only crows. Insects were scarcely to be seen […] It looked like a land in perpetual winter.'

It was during World War II that chemicals were used for the first time to control pests and weeds, the first being 4-chloro-2-methylphenoxyacetic acid. This pesticide was subsequently marketed as MCPA to farmers after the war, which ushered in the age of pesticide farming that we still have today. The growing stranglehold that chemical farming has had on modern farming methods was tightened during the 1980s, when a number of chemical companies – including Shell and ICI – bought into seed companies with the aim of breeding high-yield crops that needed high input from their fertilizers and pesticides. By the end of the twentieth century, UK sales and exports of pesticides reached £1.5 billion. The economic scale of this industry suggests that such chemicals will remain an integral element of modern farming for the foreseeable future. However, as many scientists and environmental campaigners, including the Prince of Wales, have pointed out, pesticides continue to have a hugely damaging effect on the environment.

To compound this environmental degradation, Graham Harvey notes in his study of post-war agriculture, *The Killing of the Countryside*, that between the mid-1960s and the mid-1980s, 'progressive' farming methods fully embraced nitrogen fertilizers. Their use increased by nearly 400 per cent, and by the end of the twentieth century 85 per cent of all grassland in England and Wales was being treated with artificial fertilizers. Not only does this have the effect of diminishing the soil's fauna – which in turn reduces the diversity of plants and wildlife that is part of the local ecosystem – such nitrates are the biggest pollutant of England's water supply, with approximately 300,000 tons leached annually into rivers.

With such a widespread and consistent use of pesticides, herbicides and artificial fertilizers since World War II, we have fundamentally shifted from a scene of diversity to one of monoculture across our grasslands. According to a 2011 report by the Bumblebee Conservation Trust, of the twenty-four types of bumble bee in the UK, over two-thirds have either become extinct, are seriously endangered or have become at risk during the last seventy years. Inevitably, wildlife populations have also dramatically declined. As Monbiot alerts us, a report from the UK's National Ecosystem Assessment, entitled 'Threat to Biodiversity in Wales', outlines a stark picture of the impact of modern agricultural methods.

The report shows that the decline of farmland birds in Wales has accelerated: between 2003 and 2009 the overall number of birds fell by 15 per cent. Particularly badly hit, curlews have declined by 81 per cent between 1993 and 2006, and lapwings by 77 per cent between 1987 and 1998. Overall in England and Wales, the *Farmland Bird Index* estimates that the population of farmland birds has fallen by over 50 per cent between 1970 and 2013, and only 7 per cent of animal and plant species living in rivers are thriving. The cause of such drastic changes is clearly industrial agriculture, and the report concludes that it accounts for wildlife decline in 92 per cent of cases.

It is not just the wildlife that industrial agriculture has driven from the land. As Easterbrook highlighted in the 1940s, between 1914 and 1939, 300,000 to 400,000 farm workers left the land – around one-third in total. Fifty thousand people moved from the countryside to urban areas between 1937 and 1939. Nevertheless, in 1934, 1.2 million people were still engaged in farming, and 40 per cent of farm holdings were less than 20 acres. Indeed, in the twenties Adrian Bell reversed the trend and quit the city for the country. He had his whole farming and writing life still ahead of him at this point. But it was a farming life that witnessed change on an unprecedented scale as monoculture and industrialization took hold. As a result, Bell is our eye witness and our recorder: he helps to shape our understanding of the scope and impact of the many changes on the soil, the land, the produce, the animals and, of course, the people.

The following chapters will discuss the specific changes and issues that Bell's books raise, though of course we now know that the demise of small farms is inevitable given the present direction of government and commercial interests. Current farm subsidies primarily support the intensive, mechanized practices of large farms and processing monopolies. Indeed, the Common Agricultural Policy, which currently costs the United Kingdom £3.6 billion a year, and raises the prices of feed, chemicals and machinery, is still driving small farmers out of business.

How significantly this will change as a result of Brexit is still not clear. Whilst a reform of the subsidies that farmers currently receive from the EU could benefit smaller, mixed farms whose practice is more sympathetic to the environment (something that the environmental secretary, Michael Gove has provisionally indicated), this is far from certain. As the Brexit negotiations on trade deals and tariffs rumble on throughout late 2018 and early 2019, opinion remains widely divided as to whether Brexit will be beneficial or detrimental to British business, of which agriculture is now inextricably a part. Industrial agriculture has been built on central financial support over the past seventy years. As a consequence, a lot of vested business interests, including chemical companies, processors and supermarkets, would struggle if subsidies were cut or reformed – particularly if a greater focus were placed on protecting the environment rather than simply maximizing production.

That said, away from these larger interests there is some hope that Brexit could provide a golden opportunity to chart a different course for British farming. Greener UK, a coalition of thirteen organizations – including the National Trust, the Campaign to Protect Rural England, Geenpeace, the World Wildlife Fund (WWF), the Woodland Trust and Friends of the Earth, whose combined UK membership totals almost eight million people – want to inform the discussion of the vision of farming and the environment post-Brexit, and argue that there needs to be a greater balance between food production and protecting the environment. The senior policy adviser for the Royal Society for the Protection of Birds (RSPB) believes that the two aims are mutually beneficial:

> We've always made the argument that investing in the natural environment can and does have real benefits for farming and for food production, as farming more than any other industry depends upon natural resources such as soil and water and pollinators. So it's not just about this moral case, as important as that is. There's also a really strong economic case for why you would restore the natural environment, particularly for agriculture but for other sectors of the economy too.

However, those holding out – or indeed, starting out again – are another story – hopefully a positive one for the future of smaller, mixed farms and the environment. But I'm getting ahead of myself and we need to assess the system we currently have.

The question is, if these subsidies are supporting big business rather than farming and rural communities, are they at least now addressing some of the damage that seventy years of industrial agriculture has done to the English countryside? The answer is, of course, a resounding no. Funding depends on farmers meeting certain conditions, which are laid out in an EU policy document called 'Good Agriculture and Environmental Condition'. One of the compulsory standards is 'avoiding the encroachment of unwanted vegetation on agricultural land'. Consequently, farmers receive financial rewards (Pillar 1 payments) for discouraging plant diversity. As Monbiot notes, this policy means that farmers do not even have to produce anything or keep animals on the land, 'they merely have to prevent more than a handful of trees or shrubs from surviving there, which they can do by towing cutting gear over the land.' Such procedures are so far removed from Bell's view of husbandry that it would be a travesty if it were not already an environmental tragedy.

The effect of rules such as these is, as Monbiot states, 'the frenzied clearance of habitats. The system could scarcely have been better designed to ensure farmers seek out the remaining corners of land where wildlife still resides, and destroy them.' The absurdity of such a policy is compounded because farmers can also apply for funding for 'green' subsidies (Pillar 2 payments). These reward farmers for making small changes to their land – although often just tiny corners or edges of it. Primarily this 'greening' involves crop diversification, the maintenance of permanent grassland, and establishing 'ecological focus areas' on 5 per cent of arable land.

The majority of the ideas and perspectives that dominate rural policy originate in farmers' unions, which are often governed by the largest and most wealthy landowners. Unsurprisingly, these ideas and perspectives are shaped by the subsidies that benefit large agribusinesses. Monbiot encourages us to question why, as taxpayers, we don't question this use of public funds. He writes: 'I struggle to understand why there is not more public protest around this issue. Perhaps these payments – and the rules which govern them – reflect a deep-rooted fear of losing control over nature.' I, on the other hand, am more inclined to attribute it to a 'deep-rooted' apathy about learning, knowing, and engaging with civic issues in the population at large.

Britain's present government has done little to alter the landscape of British farming outlined above. Liz Truss, the Environment Secretary of State for the Department for the Environment, Food and Rural Affairs between 2014 and 2016, was notably uninterested in environmental issues related to farming. In her address at the 2015 Annual General Meeting (AGM) of the National Farmers' Union, she made no reference either to soil erosion (the Environment Agency estimates that more than two million tonnes of topsoil are eroded each year), or to the restoration of farmland fertility, flora or fauna, or producing healthier food. Instead, she talked about technology and innovation, giving details of 16,000 new products, high crop yields, and new milking technologies. Journalist Graham Harvey notes:

Her address wasn't a speech about farming. It was a speech about the food business. It started with a hymn of praise to the industry that employed one in eight people and contributed £100 billion to the national economy. What she failed to mention was that farming contributed less than 10 per cent of this. Most was accounted for by the food manufacturers and retailers.

However, in 2008 one of the biggest studies ever undertaken of modern farming systems offered a very different vision from that of our Environment Secretary. More than four hundred scientists from around the world were involved in *The World Agricultural Report*, which concluded that 'industrial crop growing would not feed the world. It was unfit for purpose.' The report, which was funded by the World Bank, recommended that there needed to be more 'ecological' methods adopted in farming, and that – wait for it – mixed farming should replace monocultures.

The co-chair and co-author of the study, Professor Hans Herren, an entomologist and farmer, states that the industrial methods that dominate Western agriculture are not working. Not only have they led to huge environmental damage, there are a billion people going hungry and another billion overweight or obese. He believes that farm subsidies should be abolished, and that once more, farmers should get more for their produce directly from the consumers, rather than the significant majority going to the processer and the retailer. This vision for farming is one that Cobbett, Massingham and, as we shall see, Bell shared.

As this brief overview illustrates, farming in England went through a second agricultural revolution during the twentieth century. The impact on the environment, rural communities and our relationship with the land and the food it produces has been profound. Thus, when Bell made the decision to leave London for rural Suffolk to embark on a life in farming, little did he foresee that this life would lead him to produce a body of finely crafted work – beginning with his *Rural Trilogy* – that beautifully observes and honestly documents this revolution.

Suffolk Farmstead

Image courtesy of Nicholas Holloway Fine Art, Private Collection

❦ 2 ❦

PEOPLE, LAND AND LANDSCAPE:
A RURAL TRILOGY

ADRIAN BELL IS A prose poet of the highest order. His language, his images, his scenes and his sensitivity towards both the people and the land he represents, all contribute towards the enveloping sense of time and place that his works convey. Bell is also one of our best documentary historians of rural life, describing and contextualizing the seismic shift in agriculture that occurred in the first half of the twentieth century. The collection of works that introduced this observant voice and vision to the world is Bell's now classic series known as the rural trilogy: *Corduroy* (1930), *The Cherry Tree* (1931) and *Silver Ley* (1932).

Released individually at first, and then as a set, these works chart Bell's journey from his farming apprenticeship through to owning his first farm. At the same time they also document the re-education and revivification of a cultured young Londoner who seeks a more meaningful existence. Nevertheless, despite this personal perspective and narrative, Bell's trilogy is persistently focused on the ideological, sociological and political pressures affecting rural communities. Bell fundamentally questions the evolutionary ideology that assumes that change, whether through technological advances, capitalist mechanisms or political will, equates to progress. The constant refrain, therefore, in my interpretation of Bell's entire oeuvre, is his documentation of that change and its deleterious effects on the English countryside.

At the same time, Bell provides his readers with the 'who, what, how and why' that enables us fully to engage and understand the communities and way of life he seeks to portray. Set in Suffolk from 1921 to 1929, the rural trilogy may have cemented Bell's own fame as the voice of the countryside, but the process of observation and composition involved in the writing of these works also clearly shaped his own sense of individuality and purpose in life. Though his writings have been described variously as novels or fictionalizations, it is, perhaps, more appropriate to consider them as a species of life writing – that generically diverse category encompassing biography, autobiography, letters, memoirs, journals, and, of course, much of the nature writing published today.

As the biographer Hermione Lee has argued: 'Life writing is an enlightened form that pushes ahead of modern individuality. It is also refreshingly untheorized and therefore unsnobbish about what constitutes a life narrative.' Bell's works evince, again and again, such an enlightened approach, and his desire to connect the rhythms of his life with the people and the land around him makes his works a valuable contribution to our nation's rural history, as well as a powerful narrative about English individuality.

Consequently, while exploring the themes and issues raised in the rural trilogy, this chapter also seeks to bring to the fore some of the literary elements of Bell's writing which contribute to his narrative individuality. From the outset, Bell seeks to differentiate his approach from other writers associated with nature and rural writing. That is, he specifically establishes a dichotomy between an aestheticized or culturally sophisticated appreciation of nature versus an experiential one, coming down squarely on the side of experience.

Raymond Williams, in his seminal study of rural literature since the sixteenth century, *The Country and the City,* explores how writers and poets have portrayed both as symbolizing the social and economic changes in their work. In doing so, one of the criticisms that Williams levels at rural writers is that, unlike, for example, Thomas Hardy and John Clare (and I would add Bell), their vision of the countryside is often over-intellectualized, aesthetic and idealized: their vision is not grounded in an authentic experience of it. To illustrate this, he cites the *Georgian Anthologies*, which were very popular before World War I as an example of this lack of authenticity.

The Georgians, writing in the first decade of the twentieth century, settled near Ledbury and started a literary magazine called *New Numbers*. They were critical of industrialism, wanted to get away from the cities, and had an appreciation of the country and a respect for those who worked its land. However, Williams points out that this appreciation was mediated through a 'version of rural history' brought from the schools and universities of the cities. As a result, the neo-pastoral mode they adopted – often with the employment of classical imagery – meant that their engagement with the country was, however well intentioned, an aesthetic one often based on literary allusions.

Williams therefore argues that many country writers present, to a lesser or greater extent, a 'part imagined, part observed' version of rural England, which is to its detriment: 'Very few country writers in the twentieth century have wholly escaped this strange formation in which observation, myth, record and half history are so deeply entwined [...] Who then are the countrymen, within this convention?' Consequently, he struggles to find an authentic voice of the countryside in his survey of rural writers. However, I would argue that in Bell's rural trilogy, this authentic voice emerges.

Indeed, David Matless, Professor of Cultural Geography at the University of Nottingham, in his own study, *Landscape and Englishness*, examines the contribution of rural writers in mediating the countryside, and notes the extent to which H. J. Massingham, a farmer and rural philosopher who was a contemporary of Bell's, presented him as 'an exemplar seer of grounded rural spirituality', reviewing his work as demonstrating 'the transfiguration of the common appearances of the earth-life'. Massingham stresses that this 'transfiguration' is rooted firmly in Bell's practical experience: 'Let us not make the common mistake of confounding mysticism with airiness, volatility and the vagueness of the immaterial ... your true mystic sets profound and wholesome store by material things. He is the living yeast working in the dough.' Bell shares the authentic voice that Williams argues speaks 'to and for the humanity of the hedger, the thresher, the man actually altering the landscape in the service and for the gain of others'. There is a practical philosophy that runs throughout Bell's work, and he shares the 'green language' that is seen in the novels of Hardy, and in the poetry of Clare. This seeks not to transform nature, but rather recreate man – and society – in view of it.

Moreover, Bell likewise mirrors the conflict between a culturally sophisticated appreciation of nature versus an experiential one, the contest being between tradition and modernity (with the caveat that he is less anti modern than one might expect). As far as Bell is concerned, if we are to understand the land, produce real food, live authentic lives and save rural communities, then we must understand and experience the worth of the farming life. We can only do that, his books suggest, through a reinvigorated and new kind of nature writing that is experiential and individual.

Thus, Bell does not wish to offer simply an intellectual engagement with the countryside in his writing: he wanted to live and experience it. Ralph Waldo Emerson, the nineteenth-century essayist, philosopher and poet, notes in his essay *Nature*, 'what worth is there in words that have no real soil at their roots?' Bell understood this, and subscribed to Emerson's philosophy: he wanted the reader to appreciate from the opening lines of *Corduroy* that if his writing about the countryside were to have any lasting value, it would need to be firmly grounded in a fundamental experience with it. Therefore, because his observations are born out of a close relationship not only with the land, but also with others who have a similar relationship with it, Bell is able to write with more authenticity than many other rural writers then or since.

※ ※

As outlined in Chapter One, throughout the twentieth century the government in office and politics in general have consistently influenced both *what* has been grown, as well as *how* it has been grown. In 1917, just four years before Adrian Bell left London to serve his apprenticeship on a Suffolk farm, Britain's food supplies were under threat from the German U-boat campaign. In response to this, the government sought to encourage a greater level of food production by passing a bill, the Corn Production Act, which gave farmers a guaranteed price for potatoes, wheat and oats. This was good news in the short term for struggling agricultural communities, leading many farmers to increase areas of production on their land in order to take advantage of this new source of income. However, when the Act was repealed in 1921 – in less than four years – these same farmers suffered badly, particularly those who had expanded their holdings and brought larger areas of land into production. Indeed, many went out of business altogether, whilst others did not recover until there was a similar drive for production during World War II. Bell began his farming career the year the Act was repealed. Therefore underpinning his observations and narrative throughout the rural trilogy are not only the physical and emotional challenges faced by Bell himself, but also the economic and social challenges faced by the wider farming communities he was working in.

Spanning eight years of Adrian Bell's life, from the moment he decided to become an apprentice farmer in 1920 to just before he was forced to sell his farm in 1928, the rural trilogy portrays the settings and day-to-day existence of farm life in rural Suffolk. Like the majority of his work, Bell wrote *Corduroy*, *Silver Ley* and *The Cherry Tree* in a context of significant technological and cultural change. Specifically there is a sense of people becoming separated from the land as a result of the growing mechanization of farming. Whilst Bell appreciates the labour-saving benefits that such developments bring, he is also aware of some of its limitations when faced with the natural environment, and argues that 'variability only can cope with variability. Agriculture needs arms and legs.'

Bell is pointing out that the close attention and adaptability of individuals working the land must not be disregarded in favour of machinery, but he is not cynical about the changes to farming that technological advances were bringing – he is aware of how they can make a farmer's job easier and more efficient. However, he was concerned about the damaging effect they could have on the land – and on people that worked the land – if they replaced the 'arms and legs' of traditional husbandry. As the pace of agricultural mechanization and intensification increased – fuelled by the push for production after World War II – the observations and concerns that were emerging in his rural trilogy become more explicit in his later work; these will be explored in later chapters.

Corduroy, the first text in the series and published in 1930, is an account of his year-long experience as an apprentice at Farley Hall, the farm belonging to Vic Savage (Bell renamed him 'Mr Colville' in the book, so I will do likewise from here). Massingham wrote in 1951 that it is one of the most significant – and best – books to have been written about farming in the twentieth century. It is narrated in the first person and, although the names of those described in it have been changed, is essentially autobiographical. The book is loosely structured around the seasons of the year, with scenes drawn from each season to show the different challenges and rewards he experienced. It is an unpretentious and, for the most part, an unromantic account of his farming apprenticeship. However, it does introduce a greater purpose that Bell would explore more explicitly in his subsequent writing: that of natural theology. Although Bell did have religious faith throughout his life, it rarely surfaces in his writing. Instead, what is more apparent is a spirituality that he finds in the natural world, which led him to happiness and a contentment he had not previously experienced.

However, *Corduroy* may never have been written if Bell had not met the war poet and novelist Edmund Blunden, who was instrumental in providing encouragement in its writing, and practical assistance in its publication. Bell met Blunden in 1927 in the neighbouring village of Cowlinge, where Blunden was renting a cottage. This was the year before Bell was forced to sell his farm because it was no longer financially sustainable. Ann Gander, who published a biography of Bell in 2001, comments that Blunden was 'a man of greater passion and depth than Bell had ever met, who directed him towards his future path in life'.

At the time, Blunden was writing what was to become his most celebrated work: *The Undertones of War*. Although more widely travelled than Bell – he had fought in the Battle of the Somme, and worked in Japan teaching English – Blunden was keen to hear about Bell's experiences as a farmer. Gander notes that 'for once, Adrian found himself opening up about his sense of the spirit of the land, and what his life had come to mean to him. He felt that Blunden understood.' Blunden also introduced him to wider literary reading, and the works of Owen, Clare and Bloomfield had a particular influence on Bell. As a consequence of his friendship with Blunden, Bell was led to think about writing his own poetry, largely inspired by his close relationship the land.

This meeting proved to be instrumental in Bell's life after his first experience of running his own farm. Although his farming enterprise lasted longer than many of his neighbours, in 1929 Bell finally, and very reluctantly, had to admit defeat. He had farmed for a year as an apprentice to Mr Colville, then for eight years on his own, latterly with his parents. Nevertheless, although through financial necessity Bell was forced to move to a small house near London with his parents, his passion for farming remained undimmed, and he was determined to return to it.

It was during these first few months of living back with his mother that Bell began to write, and Gander notes that farming was to be his muse: 'As he sat at his desk overlooking Stour Street, the voices of women from the nearby weavers' cottages floated upon to him, transporting him back to Mr Colville's farm, and the scenes he had witnessed there [...] He was determined to recreate those scenes in a book.' In doing so, he heeded Blunden's earlier advice to him to 'write about what you know'. He was encouraged further in this endeavour by the fact that he had recently had a piece about a winding autumn lane – entitled 'A Mile of England' – published in the *Manchester Guardian*.

Bell had not kept a diary during his apprenticeship with Colville, but according to Gander, it was easy for him to recall the sights, smells and sounds of his first farming experiences: 'He recalled scenarios, trimming away the duller moments and adding humour, and the pathos of commentary' in order to ensure a purposeful narrative. Gander adds that in doing so, 'he poured in not only the pain but also the intense pleasure he had derived from learning his skills the hardest way possible, and finally he unveiled the tremendous pride he felt when he could toil alongside a country-born labourer and believe himself to be useful.'

After six weeks of writing, he finished the draft of his book in September 1929, and the first person he sent the manuscript to was Blunden. After reading it, Blunden wrote to Bell:

> There is no mistaking your book, it is excellent and various, with many curious and some powerful, imaginative passages. The wording is almost always choice, with some inclination to over-word, however, as it appears to me. I have noted on the card enclosed the few points where I would have you revise. I hope you will one day write an inquest on pastoral poets of this age, me included, in continuance of your apt comment on (Thomas Hardy's) somnambulist, but your book breaks off at such a crisis as not only makes possible but even demands a sequel someday, and there you'll frolic. I would suggest that you do not let this manuscript go without pretty good terms for its publication.

The book was subsequently published by Cobden-Sanderson, although with a note of caution that 'as most people were buying war books these days' they did not expect to sell more than 500 copies. Clearly this would not provide a living for Bell, so at his father's suggestion, he began to take on some reporting jobs for *The Observer*. It was also at this time that his father put Adrian's name forward to Robin Barrington-Ward of *The Times* as someone who could compile a crossword puzzle, a craze that had caught on in America but had not yet been introduced to Britain. Although reluctant at first, he needed the weekly income that it would provide, so he agreed, and the first crossword puzzle to appear in a British newspaper was on 1 February 1930. Fifty years later, his 4,520th appeared, to mark the Golden Jubilee of its first appearance.

Corduroy went on sale in May 1930, with a front cover by the artist Clifford Webb depicting a traditional – albeit yeoman – rural scene of horses, hounds and hunt followers in the countryside. Much to the surprise of both the publisher and Bell himself, the book sold out in weeks. Two more editions came out in the next eight months, by which time he was beginning to make a name as a writer. The choice wording that Blunden praised Bell for after reading the book's first draft was clearly appreciated by critics, dubbing him a 'poet in prose' upon encountering his work for the first time. Gander notes that he had 'an inner sense for rhythm and balance that set his syntax apart from the blank or bland. That, along with his eye for detail, and deft power of description, made his work come alive.'

It wasn't only his style that attracted readers, it was also the story he told and the themes he presented. In a time of economic distress he wrote a story of a man who, through sheer determination, escaped urban, industrial decline and struggled to become independent, working in an English countryside that evoked a better past for its population. In *Corduroy*, Gander comments further that Bell 'had written about pride, community spirit, hardworking men and women, and poor but devoted families. He talked of self-sufficiency, affinity with nature, the beauty of England. The stuff that dreams were made of in a period of such distress.' The book found an audience of people who desired an escape from the demands and restrictions of an increasingly urban, industrialized society. It provided a vision of a different way of life, where spirituality and a sense of community could be found in the countryside, which was becoming harder to be found in the city.

Despite changing the names of those taken from his own life and who appear as characters in *Corduroy*, this book is very much the account of Bell's farming apprenticeship working in Suffolk, which began when he was a young man of twenty. At this stage in his life he was looking for an escape from the path he saw that he was on, a path that had begun at the public school he disliked – Uppingham. Although Bell did not want a career in the city, and he was also unsure of other options, he did know that he wanted to write. However, as he notes in the opening page of *Corduroy*, when he expressed this wish to his father, 'he made the answer that the desire to write in the young was but a manifestation of adolescence [and] confirmed my worst fears – that there was nothing "in me" [...] as my few scrappy and turbulent compositions seemed to attest.' This paternal advice, coupled with Bell's desire to 'fly from the threat of office life' to one in the open air, led him to consider a farming apprenticeship and into contact with Colville.

As a consequence, *Corduroy* is, like any good story, a book about personal realization. From being unsure about want he wants to do with his life, the year working as an apprentice on Colville's farm provides Bell with a sense of purpose he didn't find either at Uppingham or in the city. Working closely with farmers, labourers and rural craftsman – people who had had very different experiences to his – opened his eyes to the possibility of leading a different type of life. This was a life that appeared to value the natural world and community in a way he had not seen before. The deep connection with place that he saw in the rural communities in which he now lived and worked was something he wanted for himself; however, he could see that this way of life was changing. Therefore, *Corduroy* is also about the history and tradition of rural communities. It is a book that, in many ways, foreshadows all his subsequent writing, in which he writes poetically about the practical. In doing so, he recognizes the influence and importance of the past.

The title of the book itself illustrates this. *Corduroy* refers to the material traditionally worn by farmers – it is hardwearing and warm. He notes that because clothes made of corduroy last, and because farmers are reluctant to throw away anything that might have a practical use at a later date, 'many a cottage has an interesting store laid away, usually in an old chest'. For him, these items associated with agriculture become historical artefacts as important as any other. They tell a story of the people who worked the land before him – people whom he admires for their rural wisdom and their close connection with the land. Bell writes of the farmer: 'The colours of his clothes and of the things he handles echo one another: his corduroy and the Suffolk horse he drives, his

46

handkerchief and his plough-beam. With red-blue shirt and neck cloth he rides out to the harvest-field in a wagon the colour of the sky.' For Bell, corduroy not only evokes a timeless character, it also symbolizes the growing realization that this way of life had a greater purpose than the one he left in London.

In his new environment, Bell 'wondered what earthly use my liberal education was to be to me', and was beginning to see that if such an education had had very little impact on his own personal development, he would not be alone in this. As a twenty-year old who had grown up with his family in London, Bell is fully aware that his appreciation of the countryside was very much that of a townsman, and as such was primarily an aesthetic one: 'it was but scenery to me'. He had little awareness of the agricultural potential of the landscape he saw before him, writing that 'farming, to my mind, was as yet the townsman's glib catalogue of creatures and a symbol of escape'. Thus Bell clearly acknowledges how limited his own view of the countryside was at the start of his writing career. He understood how naïve and ignorant he was, and was fully aware that in order to develop a closer connection with the countryside – and a better understanding of it – required education of the kind that he had not received at Uppingham.

In the opening pages of *Corduroy*, he readily acknowledges that he knows as 'much about beer as he does about farming', which was next to nothing. He comments further on the level of his practical ignorance at the start of his apprenticeship in an article he wrote years later for his *Countryman's Notebook*:

It had been a salutary shock to me, having just left a posh school at the age of eighteen, and gone on a farm, to find myself equated with the village idiot [...] Here my education counted for nothing, and most of it was nothing. I could have gone to Cambridge and been regarded as a brain, but here I was set to turn a handle. It was all that I was good for in the nicely ordered combination of skills whereby food was produced fifty years ago [...] sheer drudgery it was. Yes, but it was also a sweating out of former notions.

Not surprisingly, the first few weeks on the farm apprenticed to Colville proved to be a steep learning curve for Bell as he 'sweated out his former notions', and not without its frustrations. In one particular episode, Bell describes attempting to break up clods of earth with a horse and harrow, only to end up with a mess of tangled metal after allowing the horse to turn too sharply. This, together with an understandable lack of knowledge of the new environment he was in, was beginning to trouble and embarrass him: 'I was angry with myself [and] beginning to feel that I could not touch anything without making an ass of myself. [...] The men's boots seemed to absorb earth like second nature, incorporating it into their colour and character, but mine looked outraged by it.' Unlike Bell, these men had experience of working the land, which may have been passed down through generations; they had a deep affinity with it as a consequence. Bell's 'cultural' upbringing did not prepare him for the realities of working with the natural world.

However, experience often equates to learning, so as Bell develops the scene he slowly gets to grips with the horse and the harrowing and settles into a satisfying rhythm, leading him to recollect Thomas Hardy's poem 'In Time of The Breaking of Nations':

> Only a man harrowing clods
> In a slow silent walk,
> With an old horse that stumbles and nods
> Half asleep as they stalk.

In citing these lines, Bell begins to see himself as Hardy's traditional figure of rural England so often portrayed in literature and art. But with almost immediate recognition, Bell takes issue with Hardy's romanticized view of this rural figure: he sees himself as someone working with the land, not working in a landscape. In his criticism of Hardy's representation, he highlights the use of 'Only' as a word that belittles the purpose and intensity of the activity. So although Bell greatly admired Hardy's writing, he is nevertheless quick to point out that 'despite the legend of his rural understanding, [Hardy] had the non-ruralist attitude'. Bell is making a distinction between those who observe and those who do, and argues that unless one undertakes such work one cannot 'get to the heart of the matter'. He is aware that only through genuine experience can a fuller understanding and depiction of such rural 'scenes', and more importantly activities, be achieved.

For example, although Hardy suggests that the figure is half asleep and vacant, Bell's mind is in fact 'fully occupied' in the task of harrowing. He emphasizes this separation between a literary representation and something approaching a more genuine experience a little further in the passage, when he writes: 'So I was beginning to understand; and I was as busy as I had ever been in my life as I moved across the field with my horse, looking no doubt as drowsy as could be to any nature poet who happened to be passing on the road.' Harrowing clods involves focused observation, experience and skill: in short, a close critical engagement not only with ideas, but with the land itself.

For Bell, this realization was significant for two reasons. Firstly, he was beginning to appreciate the deeply connected relationship a farmer needs to have with the land that he works. He was gaining an insight into the complexity of this relationship with nature, and was in awe of the knowledge needed to make it one that benefited both the land and the farmer. In this, he is countering a common view, particularly of those who see themselves belonging to a different class from the 'peasant farmer' whom they consider as lacking a level of intelligence in comparison. Bell soon understood in his farming apprenticeship that although those he worked alongside may not have had a formal education, they had a practical knowledge that was of more value and importance in terms of community, and a thoughtful understanding of their immediate environment. Gander notes that Bell 'soon appreciated that, far from the duddle-headed peasant so often portrayed by so-called smart city folk, his country cousins were wiser in their own way than many a great scholar'. As Bell later wrote, his early farming experience blew away 'half the things that up until that time I had thought important to my knowledge of life'.

Secondly, he was also beginning to appreciate that if he was going to revisit his desire to be a writer as well as a farmer, it was experiences such as these – of a 'man harrowing clods' – that would provide the inspiration and the subject matter for his writing. Like Emerson, Bell understood that to produce writing of genuine purpose and value, it had to be grounded in first-hand experience, in the soil that he was working. Consequently, it did not take Bell long to embrace the new challenges that were facing him on Colville's farm. After the 'disconnected impressions of the first few days' that are depicted in the opening chapters of *Corduroy*, he begins to write of his enjoyment of the farm work, and begins to more fully appreciate and portray in his writing the 'idea of [his] surroundings as a whole'.

Indeed, not only is his recollection of harvesting a crop of mangolds – a root vegetable similar to turnips but golden in colour – one late autumn afternoon characteristic of many of the poetic descriptions that appear in the second half of the book and in much of his subsequent work, it also acknowledges the increasing contentment he was experiencing with this life: 'There was a glow upon us all. The sun grew large and red, became the king of the mangolds there on the horizon.' Moreover, the physicality of these daily actions was something Bell was beginning to greatly value. He was beginning to feel healthier, to enjoy his food more, and to appreciate how satisfying fatigue can be as a result of working long days outside.

This practical experience he was gaining as a farmer's apprentice would prove to have a profound impact on his writing. With the purpose of his daily actions, Bell was beginning to feel a closer connection with his environment, which would inspire and nurture his subsequent writing. Before moving to Suffolk a few months earlier, Bell had written a nature poem published in the *Westminster Gazette* – but now he was questioning both his poetic process and its outcome. His criticism of Hardy's depiction of a stereotyped rural figure extended to criticism of his own preconception of what rural life was like. Furthermore, during visits back to London, he became aware of the division between his new life and the life of those he had left in the city. At a dinner party he attended on one such visit, Bell – after listening to their preoccupations about London life – comments: 'I am the only one in touch with reality.' Bell's intention is not to be arrogant; he is simply starting to realize that, for him, significant elements of urban life were based on superficiality and artifice.

Consequently, he was also beginning to appreciate that only by being in touch with a different kind of reality could work of any lasting value be produced. In this view, Bell's growing belief was that writing should not be a purely imaginative exercise, but should be grounded in experience: 'I had come to admit that imaginative moods might not be the most important things in life [...], that the mind, to be any good, must build itself on foundations which did not exclude the dunghill.' This realization had a hugely significant impact on all his writing, and almost a decade before his first book was published, he came to believe that if a worthwhile understanding of a subject were to be presented, it must be born out of first hand, lived experience. As a result of this realization, the persistent and growing idea of the countryside as a rural idyll for those who did not live in the countryside is one that Bell explores and challenges in *Corduroy*. Although Bell, in his own ignorance, may have initially regarded his new rural life in such escapist terms, this did not last long. It soon becomes apparent that this lack of understanding, which often led to an idealised and nostalgic view of the countryside, was a damaging one.

This is illustrated when he describes, whilst out on an errand from Colville's farm, seeing a rare sight: a working windmill. He is so taken with this vision of a rural past, that he enquires after the miller. Upon meeting him, he is reminded of the miller of Tennyson's poem 'The Miller's Daughter' – he is, in a similar way to the figure in Hardy's poem, a traditional character of the English landscape. However, although Bell presents the miller in these terms, as a figure created and mediated through art and literature, he is quick to undermine his – and the reader's – romanticized view of him. Bell, expecting the miller to be very attached to his mill upon complimenting him on it, receives a reply that firmly places this scene back in the present economic reality: 'Can't say as I see any good in a thing that's out of date.' To the miller, the mill cost a lot to maintain, and was an inefficient way of grinding. In an increasingly competitive market for rural goods, the miller needed new and more progressive ways of making a living. The mill had once been 'an efficient piece of mechanism, now it was a museum piece." As we will see in the following chapters, the changes in farming practices that Bell was beginning to observe is implied in his meeting with the miller. Mechanisation and intensification of the countryside was on the horizon, and were about to alter the countryside beyond recognition.

※ ※

Those who have worked the land have, more often than not, struggled to make a living from it, and Bell was developing a greater appreciation of this early into his apprenticeship. Mr Colville's brother, Arnold, resisted following his father and siblings into farming because, as Bell describes upon meeting him: 'his earliest recollections were of his elders grumbling about agriculture, the state of the weather, the poorness of the prices'. There is a realism about the declining state of British agriculture that runs throughout *Corduroy*, and Bell does not seek to gloss over the struggle most men have to support themselves as farmers. He relates Mr Colville's recollection of farm workers striking before World War I because of low pay to illustrate the struggle they faced.

However, this struggle does not detract from the rewarding way of life that farming can offer. Rather, it creates a tension – between a pastoral escape and an economic reality – that is at the heart of *Corduroy* and at the heart of much of Bell's writing. This tension can be seen in terms of the divide between the country and the city. Thus, stereotypes persisted and fermented – those who lived in cities often viewed country dwellers as either peasants, farmers or gentlemen whilst, according to Bell, 'a person in any way connected with London is darkly important. The city paved with gold reigns still a myth of the rural brain'.

In this view, the city is regarded in more positive terms that the country; it is a place of culture, money and power. Bell challenges this hierarchal relationship in *Corduroy* and throughout his writing, arguing that this view is a largely urban construction and perpetuated by those that who have limited practical experience of working and living in rural communities. In the second half of *Corduroy*, which depicts scenes from the final six months of his experiences as an apprentice, the personal doubts and practical difficulties Bell portrays in the earlier part of the book are overcome. Bell is also discovering a sense of community, which for him was absent – or at least different – from his previous experiences. Bell could see the importance of this during his year as Mr Colville's apprentice, not least when he describes the 'flourish of life' that is a market day in April. He portrays a scene of community harmony that is almost impossibly idyllic: 'This might be the festival of spring, they laugh so together. They all seem to know one another; they meet acquaintances at every step, and long-lost friends on every corner.' Although Bell is perhaps idealizing, this evocation is a significant one – he could see that in smaller rural communities people's relationships with each other were, perhaps understandably, closer and benefited both the individual and the society as a result.

However, Bell was concerned that increasing mechanization and intensification would push aside traditional ways of countryside life forever, and these communities would begin to fragment as a result. As his year as a farming apprentice drew to a close, he reflects upon this growing realization towards the end of *Corduroy*, when describing the final day of the local annual agricultural fair:

> I took a last look back at the show as we mounted a hill; its flags, variegated as confetti, fluttered an adieu. It seemed like a ghost of some medieval Utopia, this city of white pavilions with its classic beasts and sauntering crowds. Like a ghost in its transience, too; for whoever returned in a few days' time would find here only a bare meadow, and larks singing in solitude.

In this portrayal, Bell evokes a romanticized scene in order to foreshadow the changes that were gathering pace in English agriculture. This Utopian vision of an interdependent rural life, so valued by Cobbett before enclosure fragmented it forever, was disappearing further as agriculture continued to decline. Rural communities were struggling to survive. Through economic necessity, mechanization and intensification, people were leaving the land. Bell lamented this encroaching loss and its impact on rural communities and the agriculture upon which they depended. In a time of economic stagnation and increasing desire for efficiency, he feared that this would only gather pace to the detriment of the rural population.

But Bell, in his own way, aimed to buck this trend, and rather than move back from the country to the city, he wished to make his move to the country a permanent one. His experiences during the past year, although at times extremely challenging, had nurtured his health and his relationship with the land, and in doing so clarified in him a sense of purpose. By the end of *Corduroy*, Bell sought to find a farm of his own despite the admission that he was still naïve in terms of learning the craft of farming. And so, with Mr Colville's help, Bell took possession of a small, fifty-acre farm in October – Silver Ley Farm.

※ ※

Following the unexpected popularity of *Corduroy*, *Silver Ley* was published a year later in 1931, and recounts Bell's first experiences as an independent farmer. Although it is stylistically similar to *Corduroy* in that it is written in the first person, is largely autobiographical and semi-fictionalized, the tone of it – particularly in the second half – is somewhat different. Melissa Harrison writes in the preface to a new edition of *Silver Ley*, published in 2015, that 'if *Corduroy* is all about youthful enthusiasm and the thrill of new experiences, *Silver Ley*'s subject is about the passing of time.' This is not to say it is not cheerful and humorous as he describes getting to grips with his life as an independent farmer, but as the 1920s progressed, Bell could see at first hand the impact that a declining agricultural economy was having on rural communities. And because Bell is retelling the story ten years after he first acquired the farm and has, like many others, stopped farming because of this decline, there is an added poignancy to many of his descriptions.

The growth from which farming had benefited during the World War I years was starting to wane in Bell's first year as his own master.

There were clear indications that land values and produce prices had reached their peak and were about to decline. This was something that Bell was quickly beginning to realize in his first couple of years farming. The financial and structural support that farmers received just a few years before had now been removed, and he could see the impact it was having: 'During the war years the prosperity of agriculture had been like a flower opening and spreading to the full. Now already there was a nip in the air – merchants no longer came to the stack where one was threshing and outbid one another for the corn; prices were wavering at their daring height.' In Suffolk where Bell was farming, corn was the most dominant crop, therefore any reduction in its price or demand had a significant impact. As this decline became more pronounced, so farmers looked to the government for the support that was so readily forthcoming when the country needed the farmers to sustain the war effort.

However, times had changed and centralized support for farmers was draining away, leaving them to fend largely for themselves. This was a bitter blow to farmers, who had listened to the speeches of 1918 in which politicians proclaimed that 'the agriculture of England must never again be allowed to fall into national neglect.' The most significant withdrawal of support was the repeal of the Corn Production Act in 1921, the year Bell was apprenticed to Mr Colville. This meant that farmers were no longer guaranteed a price for produce that only a few years before they had been encouraged to grow on a larger scale. Bell could see the effect that this was having on those who had invested in land, labour and machinery: more and more farmers could not sustain a living, and the government that had so greatly valued them just a few years before appeared no longer to care.

Despite the wider economic pressures that agriculture in England was subject to, Bell was nevertheless enjoying the challenges of his small farm: 'Those first few months were a buoyant time. My twenty-first birthday was just past; I was a man and my own householder. My work was about me; my fields were as private to me as my garden. My work was arduous, but my mind was easy.' Bell was living the life that he had longed for when he was cooped up in Uppingham or suffocating in London – he was not only spending his days in the open air, but he also felt that he had found freedom from the oppressive expectations and hierarchies synonymous with urban society, despite the form filling required for rates and tax returns which came with running his own business. Bell was becoming his own master and was enjoying the experience. He was, for the most part, not answerable to anybody else, and he was revelling in the sense of determined purpose this gave him – a purpose he describes early on in the book as an 'elixir':

> The air of mastery is his natural element, even though the reality is doubtful. It is an elixir under whose influence he will do double a slave's work and still whistle and sing. [...] So I have found men that were their own masters, and especially the masters of acres, employ every shift and live in the most wretched way that they might remain so. I begin to understand what at first seemed incomprehensible – why the smallholder was to be seen bent over his task in the fields [...] all the light hours they spent, in that earnest attitude, something between wrestling and praying, it seemed, for their mere sustenance; but from no human master. Oh, the ferocious independence of those men …

This 'ferocious independence' that Bell saw in those around him during his time with Mr Colville and during his first few months on his own farm at Silver Ley, was an antidote to the life he had hitherto led. He had felt constrained by the expectations and hierarchies of public school and London life, and wished to be free of them. He believed these men of the countryside were leading a less superficial, more authentic way of life in which a close connection with nature and place were the most important things. He wanted to be engaged in his work in the way that these men were; he wanted to share their 'earnest attitude' in their daily actions. Although Bell was initially an 'outsider' who struggled to comprehend the rural communities in which he now lived and worked, he was finding in farming a way of life and a culture that he felt comfortable in and wanted to be part of. This realization would define him and his writing for the rest of his life.

But this way of life was changing, with the place where Bell had fallen in love with farming becoming a potent symbol of this change. Farley Hall, where Bell had spent his apprenticeship, had just been sold to a business syndicate from outside the area, forcing the tenant – Mr Colville – to move to a nearby farm to start anew. A Mr James replaced him and was tasked with managing the farm on behalf of this syndicate, and the changes he wrought soon became apparent. His first priority was to cut the wages bill, so he sacked half the men who worked on the farm and replaced them with engines and a couple of tractors.

For Bell, this was a 'portent of the beginning of the decline of Farley Hall'. Once widely regarded as the 'best farm in Benfield', it had thrived for years as a result of Mr Colville's husbandry. But as machinery started to replace traditional husbandry – or 'high farming' – and economic pressures increased, so traditional methods of farming were increasingly being viewed as outdated and inefficient. Reflecting upon this a decade on during the writing of *Silver Ley*, he could see that this was only the beginning of irrevocable change in rural communities. Not only was the close attention and care for the land becoming uneconomic, it was also becoming impractical as labour made way for machinery. As a result, Bell observes that fields and their borders were either neglected or pressed into more intensive production:

> How this came about, and its effect on the men and their families that worked there, remains to be told. Nor does the tale concern Farley Hall alone. It came upon the whole valley in the end, till even the best farmers had to allow tangled hedges, behind which the harvest sheaves could not dry after rain, while the men had to load them wearing gloves on account of the thistles which the farmers had been unable to afford to hoe out.

For Bell, the tangled hedges and the thistles were inevitable if traditional farming methods were no longer valued. Consequently, there is an increasing tone of decline and loss towards the end of *Silver Ley*, a tone that became more pronounced in Bell's subsequent writing. He notes that although 'trade had been adverse ever since I started farming', he was just about managing to sustain his life at Silver Ley Farm, largely because he only had himself to look after. For other farmers, this was not the case. More and more were being forced to give up their livelihoods because of continuing low prices – farmers met, and protestations were made to the Ministry of Agriculture for assistance, which was not forthcoming. Farmhouses and farm cottages became vacant as Bell's rural community, like countless others across the country, struggled to survive. He recounts a conversation with his old mentor Colville, who was himself beginning to lay off men from his new farm. For Bell, this was a significant indicator of the difficult times agriculture was in, as Colville was known to be the farmer most likely to have his farm 'well manned'. Colville put it bluntly:

> The better you farm nowadays, the worse off you are. [...] I was talking to a chap in the market the other day – he's been a farmer for years, and a successful farmer. He told me he'd just sacked every man on his farm except the stock-keeper – set down some grass and let the rest grow wild. [...] And there'll be a lot more do the same if things don't show some improvement, you mark my words.

And indeed this was the case – and Bell himself was by no means immune to these worsening circumstances. He was struggling to make a living at Groveside (the nearby larger farm he had taken on after a couple of years at Silver Ley), which in 1928 led to his parents returning to London and Bell having to downsize and move back to the small cottage at Silver Ley where he had lived previously. Like Bell, his brother also wished to farm, but he notes that 'the prospects had become so bad in England [that] his uncle overseas had offered to take him to his ranch.' Nevertheless, years of farming had instilled in him the fierce independence that he had seen and admired in others almost a decade previously, and he was determined that he would continue farming as best as the current agricultural climate would allow. Farming had become his way of life, and he had no wish to consider another.

However, as the economic situation grew more desperate for farmers, and the pleas to the Government for agricultural relief continued to fall on deaf ears, Bell writes in *Silver Ley* that he received notification of a 'mass meeting extraordinary' of farmers and farm workers that was to be held on Parker's Piece in Cambridge. All those whose livelihood depended upon agriculture were urged to attend, with special trains laid on from all local rural directions. Thousands and thousands of rural workers filled Parker's Piece in Cambridge, spilling out on to the cricket lawns, Bell amongst them. The speaker who addressed the assembled crowd was the President of the Farmers' Union, but in recounting his words, Bell notes that he spoke not as a president of an institution, but as a farmer:

> We don't say much, and we are slow to kick. We like to attend to our business rather than meddle in politics. And because we don't make a fuss, we don't always get fair play. We work hard, and we want a fair living. But our barns are in ruin; our fields are full of grass; our bellies are empty. Our men, skilled in their trade, are gone from the country; their cottages fall down; they stand idle in the towns.

After several more speakers had addressed the farmers and farm labourers, a motion was agreed to petition the Government again and more strongly, that action must be taken immediately to save agriculture in England from complete collapse. However, as we shall see in the next chapter, very little changed over the next decade in terms of the support farmers received centrally. But despite the challenges that all farmers were facing, Bell ends *Silver Ley* on a note of optimism when he describes himself and his farm worker, Walter, taking a break from clearing a field of hay cocks after hay making:

> We surveyed the clear but leaden-hued sky in the warm stillness.
> 'I reckon we shall get a downfall before long,' he predicted. 'It'll be fresher when it's over, that's one thing.'
> 'Yes,' I agreed, 'it'll be better then.'

Although Bell could see that a storm was approaching and that farming in its current state could not continue, he remained hopeful that a way of life he had come to love would once more be valued as the most fundamental and essential of all human activities.

❀ ❀

The Cherry Tree is the last of the three books that came to be known as Bell's 'rural trilogy', and was published in 1932, a year after *Silver Ley*. Stylistically it is very similar to both *Corduroy* and *Silver Ley*, and like *Silver Ley*, it depicts Bell's ongoing enjoyment of farming, but also the growing challenges he was faced with in order to make a living from it. Consequently, *The Cherry Tree* addresses more directly than his previous books the deepening impact of agricultural and rural change. The continuity that binds his experiences in *Corduroy*, and to a lesser extent in *Silver Ley*, is starting to become frayed in *The Cherry Tree*. The tension between tradition and modernity is increasing, with farming subject to this tension. Bell notes towards the end of *Silver Ley* that agriculture continues to be neglected, while in *The Cherry Tree* he could see the worsening consequences of its decline all around him. He writes:

> It had died away – the old, bluff, hospitable life of the countryside – like a summer's day. I saw it fade, from the top of my stacks as I worked, or from the window of my barn. [...] The country round us became lonely, thinly populated. The old community I had known on coming here ten years ago or more was now almost gone.

The rural communities that for generations had built up around agriculture were fragmenting as many small farms struggled to survive.

The opening of the book foretells this struggle, and in doing so echoes the ending of *Silver Ley*: the storm that was approaching from the 'leaden-hued sky' is now almost upon him as its 'thunder deployed across the sky'. Instead of contemplating the hay cocks that needed to be gathered in before they were spoilt by the rain, he is contemplating an old cherry tree that symbolized changing times: 'As the years passed, the cherry tree came to be full of associations [...] to a now scattered company of strangers, friends, companions, farmers and men.' This sense of change that sets the tone for the book is once again implied through natural imagery: as Bell awakens the next morning, the storm that was threatening in *Silver Ley* has arrived, albeit in a different setting, and has brought down the cherry tree so familiar to him.

In *The Cherry Tree*, Bell depicts scenes from what he refers to as 'a time unparalleled' due to the ongoing economic pressures in English agriculture. Labour was widely cut to the bare minimum, with young men born of rural communities desperate for work, and desperate for a purpose. As 'dole days' in towns became as busy as market days, he observes that those who sought support 'wore a look that reminded me sharply of the war. One last saw it *en masse* in the faces and attitudes about to return to the front. It was the expression of those who have nothing to live for.' For generations, these men would have had significantly more opportunities in their rural communities, either as farmers, farm workers, or craftsmen and labourers of associated rural trades. The majority lived in tightly knit communities in which most grew up knowing that they had individual purpose and the support of others. These certainties were fading into memory, with nothing to replace them.

To illustrate this, Bell describes the funeral of a local blacksmith, Mark Ashen, who had recently passed away after serving the rural community for decades. With his passing also came the passing of his craft and his business, because due to the continuing decline of agriculture over the past decade, together with the increasing mechanization of agricultural practices, there was no longer a demand for blacksmithing work. This family business – this specialized craft – had ended and would not return.

So, as the mourners headed homewards, Bell observed the inevitable decline of secondary trades in small country towns that are dependent on agriculture, and laments the effect: 'The country seemed to besiege that small town, which had once been as important as the size of its church testified; Time eroded it slowly back to a village. It was a community founded upon individuality; each of its needs had once been supplied by one of its citizens.' For Bell, the passing of Ashen symbolizes the erosion of the communities of which he was once an integral part. A thriving agriculture is the mother of a thriving rural community – once this is diminished, so is everything else that depends on it.

Consequently, as opportunities to continue a variety of rural trades diminished, so did the individuality of these communities. Instead of a wide range of people offering a variety of products and services, homogenization filled the void. In place of the diversity that is the hallmark of a thriving community of individual producers and shopkeepers, he now sees a multiple store with a 'window filled mainly with tins and cardboard effigies of smiling health. Cheese is just cheese, plastic, geometrical.' It is worth remembering that this is written in 1931 – one can only imagine what Bell would think of a typical high street today.

As well as observing in *The Cherry Tree* the fragmentation of rural communities due to the continuing neglect of agriculture, he introduces a new criticism in his writing, one which he will come to revisit more vehemently in later publications. He addresses the dominant economic ideology that relegates the production of food below that of the relentless pursuit of all other 'goods'. He notes that this has the effect of simply fuelling the desire to obtain more products that are sold as being synonymous with comfort and status: 'The modern consciousness appears to me meteoric with the impetus of many generations.'

This growing culture of capitalist consumerism – which has very little to do with food – takes a stronger hold on a larger proportion of society than ever before, with traditional agriculture and the fundamental values associated with it, lost in this climate of changed priorities. However, he warns us that we foster this culture at our peril: 'Money-lust, luxury lust, and the other ingredients of ambition, fail a man late or soon [...] ultimately the earth is our only sustenance.' Instead, Bell suggests that 'surely it were better, rather than serve a life-sentence to the machine of modern amenity, to live in a hut, that one might save one's soul alive.'

Although somewhat hyperbolic in these suppositions, what underlies them is a concern for a way of living that is good for the individual and for society as a whole. He cautions that a preoccupation with

– and prioritization of – material possessions will lead to a culture of selfishness and dissatisfaction: 'I, too, have felt [...] the tyranny of the too inward mind. [...] Without the pole-star of a new simplicity, it seems to me, civilisation will continue by turns at deadlock or mad speed, like a machine out of control which bumps itself from one obstacle to another until it falls to pieces.' This 'new simplicity' is a movement back to the earth that is 'our only sustenance', not away from it, which a rising consumer culture is encouraging.

Bell therefore uses the cherry tree to symbolize the significant changes that he sees in his rural communities, and in wider English society. In doing so, he is beginning to voice a reaction against some of these changes, particularly the decline of small agricultural communities, and a growing disconnect between the producer and the consumer. So, although Bell opens the final part of his rural trilogy with the cherry tree brought down by a storm, he ends it – as he does in most of his writing – with both an appreciation of the natural cycle of life, of the past, and of hope for the future:

> But it is not yet goodbye to our cherry tree. [...] Throughout next winter he will blaze upon our hearth and be cheerful indoor company, that was our summer friend. He will be a fragrance about the cottage, putting us in mind of other days.
>
> Meanwhile a successor stands in his old place in the orchard, a shivering sapling staked against the storm.

Bell sees hope amongst shifting priorities, but only if the drift from the land – geographically, economically and emotionally – is halted and reversed. It is this reconnection with the natural world that Bell advocates in *The Cherry Tree* and, more explicitly, in his next publications: 'The Farm', an essay in *England's Heritage*, a collection of essays published by Batsford in 1935, *The Open Air* and *Men and the Fields*.

Man and Scythe

❀ 3 ❀

A DECLINING TRADITION:
THE DRIFT FROM THE LAND

THE SUCCESS OF HIS rural trilogy, along with the well-received publication of his novels *A Young Man's Fancy* and *The Balcony* (the publishers Simon and Schuster in New York requested to take on the latter), confirmed Bell's reputation as an emerging, talented writer. Gander notes that although there were many country writers around at this time, with 'some trying to emulate Bell's style', his poetic phraseology, together with his eye for detail born of his intimate knowledge of his subject matter, set him apart. Indeed, evidence of the growing status that he had attained as a rural writer was when Faber and Faber asked him to compile an anthology of rural writing entitled *The Open Air*, which was published in 1936.

However, Bell could not see a route back to what he desired to do most: farming. As the 1930s progressed, so the majority of agriculture in England continued to decline. The formation of the Marketing Boards in the 1930s did go some way to supporting farmers, and, as Harvey suggests, it would be wrong to suggest that all agriculture was on its knees: 'The truth is, the farming depression of the 1920s and 1930s was far from being the universal calamity it is now remembered as,' he writes. Rather, he suggests that: 'It was a crisis for cereal growing rather than for farming in general as a result of the collapse in wheat prices, firstly in America and then in Britain.'

A lot of farmers survived during this time due to the diversity of their production, moving away from arable crops towards grass, thus producing more meat and dairy products. However, the prices for most produce – in particular wheat – still remained low. In an area such as Suffolk where a significant proportion of agriculture was reliant on these larger crops, such depressed prices had a greater impact on the ability of farmers to sustain a living.

This was compounded by the changes to which agriculture was subject – primarily mechanization and intensification – as well as changes in wider society. For example, the drift from the land and the growth of urban areas continued as people left the countryside to seek not only work, but also a higher standard of living due to the modern conveniences that technology was increasingly offering. Instead of being a place to live, the countryside was becoming a place to escape to. Either by train or increasingly by car, it was becoming a place of leisure – a place to visit. H. V. Morton's book *In Search of England* was the most popular guide to those seeking escape from their city lives in, as Matless observes, 'pursuit of an older England'. First published in 1927, it was in its twenty-sixth edition by 1939.

During the 1930s, Bell could clearly see this desire for escape, and the influence it was beginning to have on rural communities. He notes that because of the continuing struggle to make farming a viable economic option, the value of agricultural land had fallen to £3 an acre, including house and buildings, with the price of a farm labourer's cottage between £50 and £100. However, contrast this with the £850 paid for a barn converted into a bungalow by a city dweller looking for a rural escape, and it is clear that such a discrepancy not only highlights the largely depressed state of agriculture at this point, but also foreshadows the growing economic influence of the city on rural communities.

There were others who shared Bell's concern. In 1934 the writer, poet and journalist G. K. Chesterton observed in a BBC radio broadcast:

Unless we can bring men back to enjoying the daily life which moderns call a dull life, our whole civilisation will be in ruins.... unless we can make daybreak and daily bread and the creative secrets of labour interesting in themselves, there will fall on our civilisation a fatigue which is the one great disease from which civilisations do not recover.

Chesterton is warning against a growing division between necessity and lifestyle – for him, they should be inextricably linked in a way of life. In this view, labour has an intrinsic value and an encompassing purpose, something Bell described in *Corduroy* when watching working men in the fields in an attitude somewhere between 'wrestling and praying'. However, like Chesterton, Bell could see that such 'daily life' was increasingly viewed as a 'dull life' in a society that was becoming more urban and 'modern'. This led to a separation of the values, culture and economics that were associated with the different ways of life. It is a separation that continues to influence our urban and rural societies today. This recognition of a changing countryside was one of the reasons why Bell's rural trilogy became so popular. It is also why Faber and Faber thought it timely, in 1936, to publish an anthology of country writing, and asked Bell to compile it.

As in the first decade of the twenty-first century, there was also a growing number of publications in the 1930s that regarded the countryside as a place that should be appreciated – albeit often superficially and aesthetically. One such publication was *England's Heritage*, a collection of essays published by Batsford in 1935, including essays by Bell, C. B. Ford, G. M. Young, Ivor Brown and Edmund Blunden. In the foreword to the collection, Ford wrote 'The Beauty of the English countryside owes much to the friendly care of man throughout the centuries', and the purpose of the collection was to present positive portraits of the man-made heritage of England.

As such, Ford adds that it is a 'book of appreciation, and does not deal, as perhaps it should, with the growing threat to the heritage that seems inherent in modern conditions'. Although the essays do not explicitly address the growing threat of 'modern conditions', the fact that this book was published at this time reflects a growing tension between not only the country and the city, but also tradition and modernity. One of the key concerns evident in a lot of the contributors' writing was the increasing distancing from nature, with a dominance of it, rather than a codependence with it.

Bell's contribution to this collection is entitled simply 'The Farm'. He states that the purpose of it is 'not to give a history of farming, but only to indicate the growth and changes that lie behind the word "farm" as it is understood today'. Written just five years after *Corduroy*, it provides a valuable insight to how Bell saw the changes in agriculture as compared to the way it was portrayed in his rural trilogy. One of the most significant of these changes was that, with growing mechanization, rural labour was becoming devalued. In highlighting the agricultural labourer as 'the one constant factor in our social structure', he cites William Cobbett's observations of agricultural practices and rural life in nineteenth-century England, to illustrate the labourer's diminishing purpose and status. According to Cobbett:

> The life of a labourer might be itself more instructive and intelligible than that of his counterpart, the urban artisan. His work at home and in the field afforded a more varied range of experience, in which the relation of means to ends was easily grasped. He saw the nature and meaning of his industry, often the whole processes, and their connection with social and domestic needs.

Bell shares Cobbett's view. He argues that it is a mistake to regard the agricultural labourer in any way inferior – either intellectually or culturally – simply because their life is bound up with the work of the land. Indeed, his experience is more authentic and purposeful than his urban counterpart because his work and his 'social and domestic needs' are interdependent. Bell develops Cobbett's regard of the agricultural labourer to consider how the farm itself operated in a wider context: 'There are two ways of looking at the farm and its processes, cultural and economic. Originally there was no such distinction [...] They lived entirely in the yearly cycle; and a purpose, tradition and rhythm were established among them that were a true reflection of their environment.'

However, by the mid-1930s the distinction between the cultural and economic was greater than ever before. Agriculture was becoming 'agribusiness', with the result that the agricultural labourer, once integral to the rural community, was becoming superfluous to it. With a move towards mechanization, and the continuing economic struggles in farming, the labourer's traditional roles were either being replaced or simply made redundant. Consequently, the growing divide between traditional agriculture and modern economics, and 'progressive' farming methods, meant that farms were increasingly becoming far from 'a true reflection of their environment'.

This shift, as Bell notes, also involves an altered view of our relationship with the natural world: 'In speaking of "Nature", of "knowledge", we cannot help speaking as of something outside ourselves or attached to ourselves.' This changing regard for humankind's relationship with his environment was therefore moving from one of codependency to one where man assumes dominance over it.

To illustrate this separation that new technologies in agriculture were fostering, Bell reflects how 'we only have to look at the shape of traditional farm implements to see how men's ideas followed Nature [...]; before this recent break in continuity, agricultural craftsmanship was a thing of evolution and inheritance, of which every branch was interwoven with the whole.' It is this harmony between man and nature – a harmony symbolized by the tools created by man to work with nature – that Bell sees being jeopardized by changing agricultural practices. Thus, in contrast to the synthesis between man and nature that is characteristic of traditional husbandry, Bell considers that the modern farm of the mid-1930s, with its specialization, intensive cultivation and increasing use of machinery, is 'based simply on production'.

In this context, it was becoming harder for smaller mixed farms that followed traditional methods to survive. The labour cost associated with this husbandry was increasingly regarded by farmers to be excessive, whereas the significant investment that bigger farms were making in modern technologies appeared to make sound business sense. With smaller farms failing, or being subsumed and amalgamated into larger, more specialized farms, Bell was concerned that the diversity of the countryside would also be compromised, writing that: 'It is easy, perhaps, to exaggerate the effects of these changes by the sentimental attraction of old customs; but what cannot be exaggerated is the loss of the stamp of individuality in every product of the old life.' This loss of individuality, of diversity, was highly significant for Bell because it is a fundamental characteristic of an English identity rooted in traditional constructions of rurality.

With this idea in mind, he ends 'The Farm' with a depiction of the countryside in which tradition and modernity exist side by side, leading to a new questioning of such constructions: 'In one spot we see the combine harvester cutting a thousand acres of corn, in another a man with a scythe mowing his steep half-acre; in one field a gyro-tiller at work, moving the soil like water, in another a man guiding a single plough round a rock. Nowhere, perhaps, do ancient and modern consort together so curiously.' In a small but significant way, the portrait that Bell paints in 'The Farm' explores not only changing rural communities, but also the nature of English identity and the changes to it that this agricultural revolution was starting to bring.

※ ※

The nature of England's national identity, and how significant changes in its rural heart might challenge and alter traditional conceptions of it, is again explored by Bell in his next publication, *The Open Air: An Anthology of English Country Life*. This was published in 1936 and is an anthology that Faber and Faber asked him to compile around the time he wrote 'The Farm' for *England's Legacy*.

Like *England's Legacy*, the purpose of the book is to offer an appreciation to readers of a rural England at a time of significant change. Writers whom Bell featured include many one would expect to see at the time in an English rural anthology: Hardy, Shakespeare, Clare, Jeykell, Eliot, Gray, Wordsworth and Jefferies. However, Bell also includes writers who are a less obvious choice for an English country life anthology, with

Tolstoy, Chardonne, Gourmont and Proust making appearances. With such a diversity of writers and extracts, Bell is aiming not simply to explore the aesthetic and practical changes happening specifically in the English countryside, but also to present the broader impact that these changes were having on both the individuals and the communities in which they lived.

For example, in his introduction, Bell describes sitting in a public house in an unnamed market town, 'thinking about this anthology'. He observes a contrasting scene of revelling, with 'loud men with bowler hats on the back of their heads, and pig-like large women', with a middle-aged labourer with a clay pipe 'gazing gratefully at a good fire' who possessed a 'stillness that seemed almost eternal'. To Bell, this man 'seemed the embodiment of the constant fatalistic living thread of our history; that power of quietness in him went back from generation to generation'.

In this scene, Bell is conveying a growing tension between tradition and modernity – a tension that was nurturing a readership for books such as *England's Legacy* and *The Open Air*. In contrast to the men in bowler hats, who represent a population increasingly removed – physically and spiritually – from the traditions and values associated with a rural way of life, the labourer is 'born of the earliest arts of life, of the inherited intuitive knowledge of the best way to live within the framework of natural law'. In this, Bell saw a fundamental and growing divide 'between him and the rest of England to-day', and sought to compile the anthology around this theme:

Whatever we are gaining in bath-rooms and panel dentistry, we are without doubt losing something much less easily classified. One may call it individual authority, personal sanction for living; at any rate, it is a thing of humble beginnings, of a knowledge of process and natural law. It is something about a countryman that is like the weather, something that, in a word with him on the commonest subject, gives you a vista of generations. The spark of true culture is there, which has fed the language, the music and all the arts of English life.

Although this can be viewed as a nostalgic lament for an earlier time, I would argue that Bell is evoking this vision for a different purpose. In fact, he goes some way to addressing this point himself in the introduction when he writes: 'No one, I hope, will accuse me of trying to exploit a twentieth-century nostalgia by the old dodge of the Golden Age; but what I wish to suggest is that, potentially, the countryman's home used to feed him, body and spirit, and provide him with work and recreation.' He acknowledges that technical progress, economic growth and increasing urbanization can lead to positive changes in people's standard of living, but he is concerned about what is lost as a result. He sees that such changes would lead to the separation of man and his environment: the shift from producer to consumer would diminish the modern generation's understanding of 'process and natural law'.

This growing disconnection from the traditional values associated with the countryman was leading not only to a cultural shift in English society, but also to an economic one. With a growing desire for modern, bought conveniences, 'individual authority' was being compromised, thus undermining personal independence. This was making new generations reliant upon others for their lifestyle, which is a situation Bell finds deeply troubling; he states:

> Before the tension of competitive money-making, of the need to support a certain standard of amenity, paralysed the individual life; before water and heat became commodities and the machine departmentalized and insulated vocations one from another; before the grooves of specialization became so deep that the mind was blinkered and ran in one track, the knowledge of a craft gave a man intuitively a power of judgment over all other branches of life.

In an anthology of English country life that is aimed at a general reader, Bell's message is perhaps surprisingly strong. As a farmer himself, he had lived and worked amongst others who – often over generations – had acquired this knowledge, giving them a holistic view of their life and 'a power of judgment' over many aspects of it. However, he can see that this is being challenged. Not only did specialization, mechanization and a growing culture of commodification fuelled by capitalist consumerism 'paralyse' the ability of people to lead individual and independent lives, these significant and increasingly influential factors were also forcing a separation between people at both a local and a national level. The independence and interdependence facilitated by the structure of traditional rural communities was lost, to the detriment not only of these rural communities, but in the longer term to the culture and wellbeing of society as a whole.

The cultural and economic shift that was encouraging consumerism resulted in more people becoming dependent on outside capitalist interests than on each other in small communities. Bell observes that by the mid-1930s 'the whole structure of communities is breaking up, and groping, perhaps for a wider communal unit.' Moreover he also notes, in a statement that resonates strongly amongst a twenty-first century society, that the fragmentation of such communities was compounded by evolving methods of communication: 'Broadcasting, and swift communications, give an illusory appearance of unification; they mask the real dispersion of mind that is taking place, the insulation of man from man.' Due to technological progress and shifting economic priorities, Bell could see that the investment and interest in traditional rural communities was declining.

Thus, despite the success that Bell had enjoyed during the first half of the 1930s with his rural trilogy, his publisher was beginning to question the longevity of this genre, feeling that the market for books on farming was dwindling, and so in 1937 they asked him to write a biography. Bell, however, was not keen to head in this direction with his writing. Nevertheless he did move away from the semi-fictionalized style adopted in his rural trilogy, towards a more autobiographical type of writing, based on observations and records of his immediate world.

Indeed, Bell kept numerous notebooks in the early 1930s, and continued to write these almost daily, until just before he died in 1980. They reveal a minute observation of detail, not simply of his natural surroundings, but also of his relationships with others. Perhaps not surprisingly for a farmer, these entries often start with a short observation of the weather conditions before moving on to detail the day's events. Bell offers an insight to his process of recollection:

> To me, any small daylight thing can become dreamlike by the chance of being remembered, stored like a shred of trefoil preserved, perfect and golden, in a bunch of hay dropped off the fork in being carried to the hayracks. There it lay as the mind's eye sees it, still dry, floating in a muddy puddle. All in the day's work, yet speaking something to the heart at that moment. I recall the gust which buffeted that shred of trefoil across the water in the hoofmark of a heavy horse. And that is all. Things so perishable, yet too delicate to perish from the mind.

Although, as would one expect, a lot of these entries are rather mundane in that they describe Bell's day-to-day life, there are many comments that have a wider significance. They provide a fascinating insight to Bell's thinking, and provided the raw material for the majority of his future publications. Adrian's daughter, Anthea Bell, who was entrusted with these diaries as part of Bell's literary estate, said that it was suggested after Bell's death that these should be published. However, she felt strongly that Bell would not have wanted this, as his published work was crafted for a wider audience – these diaries were his personal sketches, his *aides memoires*. Indeed, in preparation for a published collection of Bell's articles in 1965 (*A Countryman's Notebook*) it is clear that he was revisiting and reviewing these, with various pencilled edits of content, syntax, vocabulary and paragraph order.

He wrote *Men and the Fields* from observations and memories that were 'too delicate to perish from the mind' and made their way into these notebooks. The book was published in June 1939, on the eve of World War II, and on the cusp of even greater change in English life. In the foreword to the 2009 Little Toller edition, his son, Martin Bell, writes of *Men and the Fields* that: 'It is not idealized. It has no story line. It is part of the history as well as the literature of England of that time. It is a work of practical mysticism and a celebration of things as they were and would never be again.' It is indeed a bittersweet book, which not only observes the ongoing struggles of those who work the land to make a living, but also the rewards that come with this way of life. And because it is written just before the irrevocable changes that World War II brought to all aspects of English life, it is one of Adrian Bell's most significant publications.

When Bell wrote, at the start of *Men and the Fields*, 'Whatever you talk about in farming leads you back in time', he is keenly aware that speaking to farmers, observing their changing farms, and documenting their experiences, can result in nostalgic reminiscences rather than reasonably objective accounts rooted in the practical implications of a changing countryside. However, for the most part, Bell successfully avoids this in this book. He sees the gathering pace of those who live in the countryside – a pace that mechanization, specialization, intensification and urbanization were fuelling. He comments on 'how little people walk nowadays' because of the motor car, and the pressures on the 'modern farmer' to embrace new technologies and practices to keep up with his competitors if he is to maintain a living. He writes of meeting a friend whose father still walks, and who drives a horse and gig because it enables him to 'see things, [to] stop and talk to someone you meet, and thereby often have a deal – [it is] the old farming way of doing business, through social intercourse'.

It is not that Bell is being nostalgic in view of the increasing mobilization and mechanization in the countryside; it is that he understands the value of the quiet relationships and connections lost as a result. For example, he notes the 'unseen' infrastructure that was being lost due to the technological influences that the countryside was subject to:

I went on across a farm far from the road, a farm without a house any longer, but with buildings, a pond, and a lane ending in a tract of land no longer ploughed but full of bushes. It was growing dusk: at the end of the lane a man who had been hedging was making a crackling fire of thorns. He remembered cottages in the lane and a house on the farm, and the wasteland growing a crop of corn. 'It's too far from anywhere now,' I suggested. But it wasn't so far really, he said: there were foot-paths running to villages in former days, which everybody used. We think it a long way now because we always go by road, but it was quite a short distance by the paths that are now lost.

When we consider 'infrastructure', it is most likely we think of roads, bridges, schools and hospitals – largely an urban landscape. However, Bell is stressing the importance of a more hidden and subtle infrastructure that is just as significant in the countryside. The paths he describes were crucial to the functioning and survival of the rural communities – if the roads were the arteries that linked rural communities, these were the veins that kept them alive. For Bell they were not, as we might perceive them today to be, 'miles from anywhere'. For such rural communities, the centre of things was not 'elsewhere' but was very much embedded and remembered amongst these lost lanes and pathways.

Changes such as these in the English countryside brought with them increasing juxtapositions, and it is often these that have the greatest impact on Bell in his depictions in *Men and the Fields*. In order to explore this increasing tension between tradition and modernity, between an old order and a new order of rural life, he introduces the reader to various characters who illustrate these changing times, providing an insight to fragments of life in the English countryside in the late 1930s. For example, Bell recounts entering, in the spring of 1937, an oak wood called Spouse's Grove, which was just over a mile from the nearest tarred road: 'Inside the wood the ground was covered with primroses and violets, blue and white; they were in tight groups like posies at the feet of giants: just the low, delicate flowers and the tall grey trunks.' But upon returning to the wood a year later, the scene that confronted him was a rather different one:

> ... the oak trunks lay out in the field. The trees had been dragged out and carted away by tractor, and the approach to the wood was all mire and confusion. Many trunks still lay there, looking like serpents with their heads cut off. The texture of the bark seemed alive. Inside the

wood the ground where the spring flowers grew was smothered with a tangle of tops.

This contrast is further emphasized by Bell when he 'heard the sound of a saw, and in amongst these boughs discovered an old man, as though he had been caught in them and was sawing his way out'. The man, who was over seventy, lived in a small cottage a little way down a nearby lane and was cutting the felled tree-tops for his own use to heat his home. For Bell, this scene struck him as one in which two very different ways of life intertwined:

> It was strange to see this old man industriously salving a little store from the vastness of modern waste. On the one hand this old man eking out his subsistence within his small trim boundary; on the other the great machine of the economic system smashing down a host of trees and leaving the greater part of them in chaos. He was a little Robinson Crusoe, making repeated journeys to the wreck: his home was an island in an alien world.

For Bell, this man symbolizes a rural way of life that was disappearing in the face of 'the great machine of economic progress'. He belonged to a generation that, for all its struggles and hardships, lived a more sustainable existence.

This delineation is as sharp as anywhere in *Men and the Fields* when he describes his visit to the local county agricultural show. He opens this passage with a description of two blacksmiths at work in a shoeing competition, detailing the sights, smells, sounds and heat of the activity, before describing the effect it was having on those who were watching: 'Many, many people stopped there, drawn as by a magnet, only just inside the show. Several deep, they stared at the sprouting fires, at the meticulous haste of the smiths…' However, despite the intense curiosity these visitors had for the smiths, it is clear that they saw this as a spectacle of another time: it was becoming nostalgia, heritage, or, as Bell describes it, becoming a dead past of 'Old England'. Like the lost paths that connected villages, traditional knowledge – the wisdom and experience of figures from this Old England – was also being lost. Bell observes this juxtaposition of the old and the new in the people as well as in their activities.

In doing so, he identifies a difference in the way they interact with others, lacking an instinctive keenness exhibited by the old figures. He feels that scientific and technological advances in farming are eroding valuable traditional skills and knowledge, thus diminishing their interdependent relationship with the land they work. The consequences of such a dulling of the senses due to scientific enlightenment worried Bell: 'So when we have looked at the bottled animal diseases, the ambitious structures (no mere tents) of the imported feed stuffs firms, and the chemical fertilizer firms, back once again to the shoeing competition. They are still hammering away as though life depended on it. Perhaps it does.' Here, Bell is holding the past, present and future together in order to illustrate these changes, whilst warning of the negative impact that growing intensification and mechanization is having on the countryside and the individuals that live there.

To develop his theme, another figure Bell introduces in *Men and the Fields* is an elderly woman who lives in a small room at one end of an isolated farmhouse situated at the end of a long muddy track. This room is linked to rest of the house by only a small, child-size door. The current owners of the farm – who are now elderly themselves – have no idea how old she is, but they do know that she was 'bought with the farm' and has outstayed the three previous owners. She does not ask for or receive any wages, but without instruction or requests from the owners, feeds the stock from her own door that leads to the yard. Bell describes meeting her on a visit to the farm:

> She looked like an animated sack with a hat on top: her face was entirely hidden by it. [...] Her father had been a farmer here. When he died she stayed helping on the farm and looking after her mother.
>
> 'People were always on to me to go away when my mother died,' she said, 'but I wouldn't.'

'You're content up here?'

'That's right, I content myself. I never wanted nothing else.'

[...] 'The nights must seem long. What do you do all the time?'

'I find plenty to think about,' she answered, swinging the sack of food on to her shoulders. 'I think about these.' She nodded her hat towards the bullocks and pigs.

Bell greatly admires the sense of contentment that is evident in this old woman as she offers a simple contrast to a world he could see becoming increasingly materialistic and discontented – locally, nationally and internationally. As he reflects upon her seemingly simple existence, he writes:

[...] As we drove home, and darkness came on, I found myself still wondering about her: sitting in her room with all the night before her, thinking of the animals. What has left me with such an impression of ruddy light about that glimpse of her face? Had it been caught at that moment by a gleam of sun, as she turned, smiling to herself, and went into the dim bullock yard?

This woman made a lasting impression on Bell, as she appears to embody some of the values that he saw were being lost in a changing society: a clear sense of purpose, a fundamental connection to place, and a deep sense of contentment without material goods.

Bell illustrates the loss of such values with a further example when he describes entering a village to ask the local shopkeeper directions. The shopkeeper was originally from the village, and was always eager to meet strangers, particularly if they, like Bell, were farmers. The shopkeeper had worked on a farm as a boy and had very fond memories of his time spent with the animals and the men on the farm. During their talk, the shopkeeper observes that this community he had grown up in had now dispersed – the farm was given to grassland, and the hop-pickers were gone. With the development of roads and transport, people had left the land to go to employment in road haulage and bus driving.

Although he admitted that progress was benefiting his own business to a certain degree, he felt it came at too great a cost to the wellbeing of the local community, and, as Bell observes, to the shopkeeper himself: 'The land no longer produces what it did; the people no longer eat the bread of their fields; the windmills are gone; and that touches him at a depth beyond the assessment of conveniences. He is afraid.' Bell notes that he sees this fear in a lot of 'country people, deep down' as patterns of life were challenged and changing. However, this is not simply fear of the unknown. Rather, it is more a fear of what is being lost, striking at the heart of both individual identity and of rural culture.

Moreover, it is not only in the rural communities that Bell observes this challenge to identity and traditional culture. Recounting a recent day out in Sussex to a small market town called Rye – a town in which, Bell notes with dry humour, Henry James used to live – he writes that 'Rye is positively frightening: it is like a ghost, like a skeleton with its ribs painted.' Bell is observing the diminishing of the town's identity due to a fragmentation of its community. He notes how the stallholders that sell local produce in small market towns such as Rye are struggling to survive due to the increase in the opening of shops that he describes as mere 'depots for trusts and combines'.

What is left as a consequence is, as Bell notes, 'a façade to people who are out of their context of living'. Bell is witnessing a change in ideology, one that is inextricably linked with a growing consumerism, which prioritizes an ideal of independence over a sense of community. The focus of this ideology was, as far as Bell could see it, increasingly on the individual with a spurious notion of providing freedom and choice rather than actions that would sustain and benefit society as a whole.

Bell provides a further example of the fragmentation of functioning communities when he describes meeting a tramp on a visit to the town of Winchelsea. This man, who is seventy-three, cycles from one village to the next and sleeps under hedgerows – he was en route from Dover to Hastings when Bell encountered him. Bell asks him how he came to live this life. The man replies, with little hope for the future: 'After the war, nobody didn't seem to want you, so I got into the way of travelling – and now I can't stop. I go all over the country on that thing. And at the same time, if you understand me, I'm fed up with it. I really shouldn't mind if I was dead.'

After the old man had finished his sandwiches and had left Bell on the grassy bank in Winchelsea churchyard, Bell was again struck by how our rural communities did not appear to serve the interest of those who lived in them: 'I was feeling like shouting – that the land everywhere was neglected, and the country turned to a holiday camp, and people like him with nothing to do.' In both the country and the towns that were familiar to Bell, he could see a superficiality beginning to subsume subtler values in which appearance and individualism were negatively impacting people's relationship with the land and each other. Bell could see that this commodification of land and town, in which relationships were becoming increasingly dominated by financial concerns, was beginning to create divisions in society that would only widen over time, and lead to greater inequality and disenfranchisement.

Despite the intentionally fragmentary and somewhat disconnected nature of these portraits, underlying Bell's observations is a common theme that runs throughout *Men and the Fields*: the decline of farming that had taken place throughout the 1920s and 1930s. This impacted not only those who worked on the farms, but also the trades and crafts that served an agricultural community. Although farming would prosper again as a result of government intervention during World War II, after almost two decades of decline, agriculture was at this time in a parlous state.

Bell depicts this decline by recounting three encounters with farmers during a holiday in Devon. The first farmer, who now gardens just a few paddocks in Lynmouth, used to own a large farm in the West Country, but was forced to sell due to the rising costs and declining prices for his produce – particularly for wheat after the government withdrew guaranteed prices with the repeal of the Corn Production Act in 1921. The second, who farmed some of the highest land in Exmoor, deeply appreciated his connection with the land he had farmed all his life, but said 'If I had my time over again, I wouldn't be a farmer, though I love it.

There's no living in it now.' He further explained that some of the fields that he had worked so hard to cultivate for production are now going back to wasteland as it is becoming more profitable to have paying guests in the spare rooms in the farmhouse.

The third farmer he meets is in Ely in Devon. Bell describes the initial impression of the farm buildings, and elucidates the beauty inherent in their form and functionality: 'They have a haphazard look that is called picturesque. They were built so, some would say, haphazard, but I don't believe it. Nothing is done haphazard on a farm.' However, Bell also observes the changing context in which they now stand. The building of modern council houses would involve endless 'planning and committee-ing, proposing and postponing', which the buildings he sees before him were not subject to. Such bureaucratic procedures highlight the growing separation of process and outcome, which makes farming increasingly challenging – if not impossible – for these men and their families.

Due to changing social, economic and cultural influences, Bell is observing and documenting through these encounters a time of altered expectations amongst the individuals at the heart of these rural communities. As Bell takes leave of the farmer, his buildings and his land in Ely, he asks the reader to challenge their own preconceptions of those that live in rural communities: 'Go all over that house, the great buildings, the fertile slope of valley; listen to him as he tells you of his father and their family there, then lays a hand on your arm and tells you what his ambition is for the future – a bungalow on a bus route and half an acre of ground.'

For this farmer, and perhaps other farmers, they will be able to reconcile their old life with their new one and adapt. For many other farmers, this is not the case. The gradual decline of their farms due to growing economic factors ultimately leads, like those above, to foreclosure and the sale of their farm. Bell could see that no longer was the stewardship of a farm passed down from one generation to the next, and suggests that for them it is a 'sort of death: as real as death of the body. A farmer who has farmed all his life – out of a farm, what is he? Time has lost its rhythm for him: it is mere duration.' Whilst such cases are individual tragedies, the effects of them ripple outwards and impact the wider rural communities of which these farmers and their farms had been a vital part for years.

As a consequence, Bell sees the impact that a changing economy is having on farming communities such as these. Not only are they subject to the pressure of increasing competition to reduce costs in order to provide cheaper prices for the 'consumer', but this rising culture of commodification forces more and more people 'out of their context of living' in order merely to subsist. It is a movement away from a local economic context to a national and, increasingly throughout the second half of the twentieth century, an international one. This concern was shared by Wendel Berry, writing in response to similar changes he had seen in rural communities in America around the time of World War II:

> Thus the estrangement of the consumer and producer, their evo-
> lution from collaborators in food production to competitors in the
> food market, involves a process of oversimplification on both sides.
> The consumer withdraws from the process of food production, hence
> becomes ignorant of them and often scornful of them; the producer no
> longer sees himself as an intermediary between people and land – the
> people's representative on the land – and becomes only interested in
> production. The consumer eats worse, and the producer farms worse.

In this context of widening economic influences in agriculture, the wisdom and experience of the three farmers above provide no profit or hope for the future, so are swept away, their land becoming something that is to be exploited for production at the expense of the traditional purpose and values of the local community. To compound this, the trades that are focused in towns and cities become so far removed from those based in the countryside, that those 'who follow them live a life among themselves'.

Bell ends *Men and the Fields* with a description of a market town that brings into sharp focus this separation of town and country, and of producer and consumer:

Coming out by by-streets into the centre of the town, I am conscious of a world of difference. Here the electric light falls everywhere on tins and boxes and wrappers – a bewildering scintillation of fancy goods. It is quite surprising to remember that this great open space is called Market Hill. Once cattle and pigs and ducks and geese were sold here, that are now tucked away in the little sale-yard among back streets.

Bell could see the marginalization of local producers, tradesmen and shopkeepers by the growing influence of bigger businesses. In this, any real chance of social or environmental sustainability – for either the consumer or the producer – is severely compromised. It is the division between the consumer and producer, and the undermining of this relationship, that Bell arguably laments above all else in *Men and the Fields*. Look to your local High Street today to see how far removed we are now from those who grow the food that we eat. Bell recognizes in his honest and poetic snapshots of rural and town life, that it is an estrangement that must be addressed if our relationships to our land and to our wider communities are to be repaired. It is a recognition that he explores more explicitly in his next two publications: *Apple Acre* and *Sunrise to Sunset*.

❀ 4 ❀

A COUNTRYSIDE WORTH FIGHTING FOR

THE CHANGING RURAL COMMUNITIES that Bell presents in *Men and the Fields* were brought into even sharper focus with the imminent threat of World War II. In the light of this threat a growing number of publications looked to the English countryside with a renewed appreciation of its purpose and its beauty. One of the reasons for this was that English identity – the England that was being defended – was predominantly conceptualized in rural, not urban terms. In this pastoral vision, more traditional forms of existence were becoming valued again: self-sufficiency, local communities, the valuing of precious resources. As had happened after the declaration of war in 1914, the countryside and those who worked in it took on new importance for the nation – its people had to be fed.

The indifference with which the government and the wider population had regarded farmers during the 1920s and 1930s, which had led to the decline of agriculture that Bell witnessed and documented, primarily in his rural trilogy and in *Men and the Fields*, was suddenly swept away in a call to arms for self-sufficiency. There were rapidly growing concerns that plentiful food in Britain could no longer be taken for granted. It became worryingly apparent to a largely urban population that the lack of support English farming had received since the end of World War I meant that the country had become reliant on importing a significant proportion of its food, and would be unable to feed itself if war led to a cessation of these imports.

Man with Cap

Publications such as Lord Lymington's book, *Famine in England* (1940), exemplified the situation the country found itself in, and agriculture was once again looked to as being critical to people's lives. The famous slogan 'Dig for Victory' and the associated campaign was the call from the Minister of Agriculture for everyone who had a plot of land to grow food for the war cause. The appreciation that the general population – and policy makers – had for farmers and the countryside had, very swiftly, never been so high.

In *The Changing Village*, published in 1939, F. G. Thomas notes that, as a consequence, contemporary literature reflected a growing rural sentimentalism. This appetite for countryside writing was one that Bell's publishers had only a few years previously suggested was waning. However, such writing was once again becoming popular, with a variety of books – along with daily and weekly publications – increasingly concerned with the technical and social issues of the countryside. Thomas writes:

> In such ways a large public, vitally interested, can live vicariously, if only for a moment, with the people of the soil, who themselves are pictured as living wholly and creatively. Underneath the townsman's sentimentality is a basic and true sentiment for reconciliation with living things. [...] The sentiment is there and can be capitalised on in any planning for the future. This is of importance, for civilisation is a thing of the spirit, and the human spirit needs contact with Nature. This is a truth of individual and social experience. This need is more than desire: it is a primeval necessity for man.

One of the most popular books that fed into Thomas' observation that 'the human spirit needs contact with Nature' was *Countryside Mood*, a collection of essays from various country writers including Bell, Massingham, Pitt and Williamson. In his foreword to the book, the editor, Richard Harmon, writes: 'In an age of destruction there is a re-awakened interest in all things that endure. The hills, the fields and rivers of England touch the hearts of all of us because they offer normal living and the natural joys of the earth. Life is very much more real and full as we get close to the earth.'

In this new appreciation of agriculture and the countryside, rural writers such as Bell found a new audience. Indeed, because of the continuing popularity of his rural trilogy – *Corduroy, Silver Ley* and *The Cherry Tree* – Bell was seen as someone who could articulate the importance of farming to a wider audience in order to rally people to dig to victory – so much so that, in 1944, he was asked to give a talk on BBC radio immediately after the nine o'clock news on the subject of 'The Land'. Furthermore, in light of this broadcast, he was asked by the Bishop of Lincoln to speak in Lincoln Cathedral on the same subject. Bell notes that such instances 'show how the nation's spirit and its agriculture were integrated at the time of stress'.

This reawakening 'at the time of stress' gained significant momentum, with *Countryside Mood* reaching its sixth impression in just over two years. Bell's contribution to the book is an essay entitled 'Meeting a Man with a Horse-rake', in which he considers the renewed focus and value placed on farming in wartime with a sense of pride for the way of life that he not only loved, but believed was fundamental to the future of a post-war England:

> As I journeyed yesterday through the lands of a large estate [...] not only the fields, but the woods, the hedgerow timber, every tree, had a look of being tended. All had a sober yet singing order that was like art; it was art, the greatest. And the horses, harrows, drills, tractors, moving about the landscape were its breathing and its life. It was a picture that drew the past to the present, both were knit in it. The great estate, its every house a home, integral to it, seemed to me then England's very nature.

In *The Unsettling of America*, the farmer and rural writer Wendel Berry explores the construction of rural culture, which is akin to the 'very nature' that Bell identifies. Berry argues that this culture is an 'inescapable kinship between farming and art, for farming depends as much on character, devotion, imagination and the sense of structure, as on knowledge.' For him, like Bell, farming is a 'practical art'. Therefore Bell's vision of a timeless rural practicality, in which man works in such harmony with his natural world that it is elevated into some kind of art, is a response to both the fragmentation he identifies in *Men and the Fields* and the impact of war. For Bell, it was a time that 'England's very nature' – its character, its structure, its knowledge – was at threat from within and without, which is a theme he develops in his two books published during World War II: *Apple Acre* and *Sunrise to Sunset*.

After his rural trilogy, *Apple Acre* is Bell's most popular book both in terms of contemporary readership and its lasting appeal. Bell's opening words go some way to offering an explanation as to why it was so popular, and why it endures today: 'This book is a picture of an English village in wartime. It was written in the early days of the war against Nazi Germany, before what Churchill called "the end of the beginning", when the tide had not yet turned in our favour.' Thus entwined with the most significant deadliest war in the twentieth century, Bell sketches portraits of a countryside undergoing irrevocable change. In these portraits he develops some of the themes presented in *Men and the Fields*, whilst introducing others. For example, he continues to advocate small-scale husbandry in a context of larger scale mechanization and intensification, and stresses the importance of maintaining thriving rural communities. He also argues that rural craft is a fundamental contributor to rural culture, and how a rising consumer culture is undermining this.

Bell did not consider that *Apple Acre* would be published as a book. That is, he did not conceive it as a whole. He notes that it is a series of observations made over time: 'I merely scribbled a sort of diary at the end of days.' Bell is perhaps being a little disingenuous with this comment: his fine crafting of language is as evident in these observations as it is in any of his work. And, although there is a lack of the more formal overall narrative structure evident in his other books, this does not compromise its effectiveness in his depictions. Indeed, the fragmentary nature of his 'scribbles' adds to their immediacy and authenticity.

Despite this sense of fragmentation, the text still charts a life – this time a life of rural communities. In *Apple Acre*, Bell traces a year in the life of a village, reflecting more explicitly than in any of his previous work a way of life under threat from a variety of national and international, social, political, economic and cultural influences. In these observations, Bell wanted to document the effect of these larger influences on a community, and the possible impact that war may have had on them and the countryside in which they lived.

Although there are few direct comments about World War II in *Apple Acre*, Bell nevertheless reminds the reader that, underlying the normality of life – of which he provides glimpses through his portrayal of various rural figures – is the threat that this life will be forever changed because of it. Bell writes: 'Then we hear the guns. Dull and sullen, they sound all afternoon, while we plant trees in the sun. Nora takes the children to the post, walking slowly along the sunlit road to the boom of the guns.' Bell juxtaposes ordinary moments from his immediate life with the extraordinary, to highlight the tension of the times in which they were living. For example, he recollects that his daughter (Anthea) shared her fourth birthday with the escalation of World War II: 'Anthea's best day – and the world's worst. The Germans blasting their way into France – Anthea waking early and telling the twins, "I'm four years old today!"'

Although such specific observations of the day-to-day impact of war may be infrequent and often implied, they are nevertheless never far away in Bell's writing during this period; there is a wider context to his observations that is largely absent from his earlier work. This can be seen in a description of a mid-winter's twilight journey that Bell took towards home:

The trees become silhouettes, the sky is all bruised light. There is no wind. Smoke creeps out of a cottage chimney. Sheets are frozen stiff on the line. A farm exhales its odour, that is its soul, and wraps us up in an aura of old England. It is a smell that even seems to have warmth, the air is so scaldingly cold. Puddles in the empty yard glitter: the shapes of the buildings have a look of permanent purpose.

The poetic nature of this vision of 'Old England' – and the tone of it – is understandable at a time of war. It is mid-winter, and life appears to be resting, almost absent. However, the 'smell that even seems to have warmth' provides comfort in this scene – its familiarity is reassuring. But Bell is also suggesting something else here: in this scene lies the essence of the country's identity – what he describes as 'the spirit of England'. The values that are being defended and fought for were not forged in the cities, but have been created through the fundamental relationship between its people and its land. It is not just the farm's soul that Bell can feel on this cold winter's twilight; it is the soul of England.

In his 1964 foreword to a new edition of *Apple Acre*, Bell writes that as a result of the threat to England's 'soul' there was a renewed focus on self-sufficiency, and notes that 'this concern for the home-grown and the home-made was one of the conditions which gave a tone of emergency to the writing in this book.' Bell observes that with the onset of war, people looked to the countryside with an altered perspective. Throughout the 1930s he had witnessed the growing disconnection between the urban and the rural, between the people and their land, and he strongly believed that such a disconnection was fundamentally damaging to both the population and the environment. However, with the threat of war upon them, England's urban population viewed the countryside with a new-found appreciation.

Moreover, not only was the countryside a place that would produce the food that would sustain the nation in its fight against the Germans, it was the countryside, not the city, that symbolized what was being fought for. He writes: 'The image in which we saw this England was made up of its beauty, its fruitfulness and its traditions: it was typified more by an old town like Lavenham than industrial Sheffield.' Once more, Bell is suggesting that English identity was constructed with reference to a vision of rural, not urban England. Despite the circumstances in which *Apple Acre* was written, Bell appreciated that there was a renewed focus on the countryside, and an increased regard for it from the wider population. After years of decline, both for him and for others who had struggled to make a living from agriculture in a densely populated country, it was welcomed and needed that the countryside – and agriculture in particular – was being appreciated and valued.

But in *Apple Acre* it is not just war that Bell sees as a threat to the 'spirit' or 'soul' of England. He also sees that mechanization, together with scientific advances, is undermining a farmer's connection with his immediate environment. He writes:

> Fifty years ago farmers were engaged in as competitive a battle to make farming pay as now, yet a lane like this to a child was a world in itself – and not only to the child. I wonder if farmers today have time to sit and watch fox cubs at play? [...] One farmer the other day expressed regret to me that he seemed to have little time to enjoy nature. So much rethinking has to be done continually in the light of scientific discoveries that the progressive farmer's mind is full of chemistry and the pros and cons of rival techniques.

Although there is a nostalgic tone to this passage, it nevertheless exemplifies the reality of the significant changes that farmers were experiencing in agricultural practices previously outlined. 'Progressive farming', which was inextricably linked to the interests of business, demanded that farmers re-evaluate traditional methods of farming in favour of methods that required investment in new machinery and technology. As well as being producers, farmers were becoming consumers. From tractors and implements to chemicals and new types of crop, they were increasingly told by the marketers and advertisers of a growing agricultural industry that, to survive, they needed to challenge their traditional practices in order to adapt to this necessary, progressive farming.

In *Apple Acre* he saw that progressive farming meant an increasing capitalization of the land through significant investment in machinery and artificial fertilizers, and questioned the benefit these changes would have on the land and on the people who worked it. If there is – or was – such a thing as 'the spirit of England', a respect for the earth beneath its people's feet was elemental in its creation. Instead, he saw a growing commodification of the land, driven largely by those in business who had a financial but not an emotional (or spiritual) investment in it. For Bell, an enjoyment of nature comes only with an appreciation and respect for it, and he feared this was being lost.

Bell opens *Apple Acre* with a series of list-like observations in a chapter entitled 'You Would Hardly Notice It'. In them, he offers very brief portraits of individuals or events in an unspecified village. In doing so, he is exemplifying the values that are inherent in traditional farming communities, values that have often been overlooked in recent times. The opening paragraph depicts individuals who make a living either directly from the land, or as part of this rural community:

> One has pigs and a little wood. Another has an orchard and fowls. Another is a wheelwright, with a vine growing up his workshop and a fig tree on his house. He also has four cows. Another has a horse, an ass and (their offspring) a mule: with this team he ploughs an acre here, an acre there: on one acre he grew eighteen coombs of wheat. Another, old now, a wagoner in his day, has a double allotment on which he grows mangolds, filling a hamper with them, barrowing them to the roadside where a farmer's cart collects them; forty hampers filled to a load. Another has kept a family on four and half acres.

Though we get an immediate impression of industry, productivity and diversity in this depiction, Bell offers no explicit explanation or comment on these individuals themselves. But what can be inferred from the portrayal of this rural scene are themes of community and independence. It is also clear that each figure in Bell's landscape has an interdependent and sympathetic relationship with their immediate environment, and embodies the values that Bell subscribes to.

Prisoner of War (POW) letter from Private Arnold Walter Coombe addressed to Bell (10 June 1943, Italy). Coombe was keen to tell Bell how much his rural trilogy had evoked a vision of rural England. He writes that, 'to have been brought back to the simple, natural, intimate things of life has been a most grateful experience, though it has increased – oh! almost unendurably – the desire to see England.'

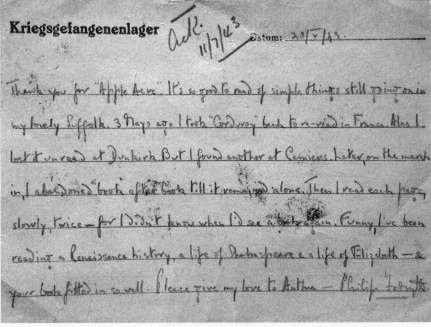

A letter from Philip Forsyth, stationed in France, 23 [May] 1943. He writes: 'It's so good to read of simple things still going on in my lovely Suffolk,' and notes that, although he abandoned book after book 'on the march', *Corduroy* remained with him.

The second observation is another brief portrait of an individual, but this time a gravedigger, and it has a different tone: 'Another who digs the graves tells of the multitude buried in this earth. He knows the veins of soils, as he digs himself down out of sight into rock clay. Once, down there, he found the perfectly preserved body of a little girl.' Bell deftly links the working of the land with the classic image of returning to the earth – the gravedigger's life. 'The veins of soils' are the source of all life and growth, and it is where everyone will return to. This imagery is further developed in the next paragraph when Bell describes the scope of another rural figure's work – a wheelwright:

The wheelwright's yard has flashing red ladders at harvest, while within, a coffin is in preparation. It lies there like a person whom the wheelwright in his spectacles and with gentle hands is tending, filling every flaw in the clear flesh of planed wood. This to be lowered into the earth: the ladders to step strong men up to the top of their stacks.

The image of the red ladders, enabling 'strong men' to carry out their work, symbolizes life at its most potent: men at the peak of their physical powers working with the land to provide for others. The coffin 'to be lowered into the earth' is where these men will ultimately come to rest. In these extracts, all taken from the opening page of *Apple Acre*, it is clear that Bell is not only valuing the seemingly mundane day-to-day activities of rural workers, but also presenting the cycle of life he is seeing all around him. He is valuing the lives of those he lives amongst, and in doing so, is acutely aware of the fragility of these lives – particularly at this time of war. The contrast he presents in these opening depictions highlights the transient nature of existence, but without passing judgement. As Bell often does in his writing, he alludes to wider themes and ideas, allowing his reader to interpret his observations.

However, towards the end of this short opening chapter, these allusions become more direct as Bell becomes critical of the influence in rural communities of outside bureaucracy and economics. As a result, Bell's portrait of this village becomes clearer as he takes a step back from the individual figures depicted above: 'Sometimes you move a heavy stone and are surprised to see creatures living a hidden life underneath it. [...] Under the weight of mass legislation an unregarded but persistent local life goes on. It is not recorded in forms, it cannot be seen by the visitant or passer-by.' Bell suggests the way of life in this 'hardly noticed' village is being threatened by outside influences – in this instance, the increasingly dominant culture of centrally driven policy-making and mass legislation.

Consequently, it is a portrait of contrasts. Whilst local craft, knowledge and community is symbolized by Bell in a wheelbarrow in the parish 'that is a hundred year old' and still fulfils its original purpose, he also sees that wider 'progress' in society has led to neglect and poverty here: 'Electricity passes through the village, but none of the cottagers can afford to have it. There is no post office, school, parish hall. Every cottage, save about three, has been condemned.' Although Bell acknowledges that there is a renewed appreciation of the countryside, he is also aware that the way of life these villagers have led for generations is, ironically, becoming more challenging in such a rapidly changing society. Bell is arguing that mechanical and technological advances, together with an increasingly homogenized and consumer culture, are suffocating small communities such as these.

Indeed, the growing influence of technological advances, wider legislation (primarily introduced through the War Agriculture Committee) and changing farming practices in rural communities becomes more apparent in a further observation in *Apple Acre*. Bell describes a day lifting beetroots with Mr Prinker. Mr Prinker, who previously worked on a large local estate before war taxation forced the estate owner to lay him off (along with fifteen other men), now has a small nut wood and twenty pigs. Bell respects the deep relationship Prinker has with the land and his animals, and the meticulous way he believes they should be managed.

For example, Mr Prinker is critical of the modern restrictions imposed on farmers, which damage the traditional husbandry of generations. Specifically, he objects to the food he is encouraged to feed them – 'I never did like bought food, you don't know what's in it' – and

97

which is far removed from what they would eat in their natural wooded environment. He also objects to merely 'fattening' his pigs and selling them 'en bloc' – he sees this intensification as bad for pigs, the farmers and the consumers: 'I believe,' says Mr Prinker, facing the sun, 'in home-fed pork. I mean, barley like I used to buy off Mr Camm – and then you've got something that'll stand up to your knife.'

For Bell, Mr Prinker's words are significant because they encapsulate the fundamental elements of a way of life that he has always valued, namely small-scale independent husbandry in line with organic principles. Although Bell can see these elements are slowly being lost due to changing economics and farming practices, he remains optimistic that the practices of farmers such as Prinker will not be wholly subsumed: 'I am cheered by the tenacity with which these countrymen cling to the values of things when the things themselves are lost. That phrase about meat standing up to your knife, for instance; a whole rule of husbandry is hidden in it.'

It is this rule of husbandry that is being increasingly challenged by modern agricultural practices, and he fears that this will lead not only to environmental concerns, but will also be damaging to wider society. Bell echoes Prinker's rural ideology when he notes that 'the spade is the microcosm of husbandry' in that it involves man, on his own or in collaboration with others, working in close relationship with the land. As soon as this relationship is broken, through mechanization and artificial intervention, people become separated from it physically and, more importantly, emotionally. The land becomes something dominated and utilized. In such an approach there is little regard for what is being lost in the advocation of 'modern' and 'progressive' farming methods.

For example, the idea that mechanization is good for the farmer is questioned when describing a conversation with a nearby farmer, Mr Winch. Mr Winch notes that the neighbouring farm, Magpie Farm, has just been bought by a young man from abroad who 'wanted to get on with mechanized work'. However, Bell observes that Mr Winch is sceptical that such mechanization will be beneficial to the young farmer. He cites how his son now works 'twice as hard as he ever did' despite using a tractor that was supposed to 'save labour'. Although Bell admits to being a little wistful and nostalgic, this nevertheless leads him to reflect how 'peaceable and smiling' Mr Winch's hard hand labour appeared to be by contrast, and how the creeping mechanization of the fields causes not just an emotional disengagement with the land. Bell writes:

> I, too, feel happy in the mud here trying to slice off the top of a beet with one chop, without wasting any of the beet – by no means easy: trying to scrape off the glutinous mud, thinking, that's good earth to be washed down a factory drain. I hate to think of it going down the factory drain, when it ought to be fostering barley seed here next spring.

This is another important observation by Bell regarding the consequences of mechanization: the craft of the farmer is increasingly devalued, the close relationship he has with his land is being undermined, whilst the earth he farms is being washed away. He is acutely aware that further mechanization will lead to unprecedented intensification, which may cause unknown damage to the land and beyond. By highlighting the consequences of farming methods that are fundamentally different to those that have been practised for centuries, Bell is foreshadowing one of the most significant environmental challenges we are faced with today: soil erosion.

The loss of rural craft also concerns Bell because it is a fundamental characteristic of rural workers' close relationship with the land in which they live and work. Although he does not explicitly refer to it as a 'craft', Bell often returns in his writing to the skills and knowledge that a farmer – or any rural worker – must possess. An example that illustrates the complexity involved in something that, without experience or knowledge would appear the simplest of tasks, is, as Bell calls it, 'the management of ladders'. He explains how any rural worker:

> … will have to learn the management of ladders: how to foot them round and coax them deep into a tree without breaking the branches. And how to carry a forty-staver in a wind, making a pause between

lifting it on the shoulder and starting to walk, to get the balance of it. And how to carry a ladder up a ladder, when you want to mend a roof. In fact, the whole art of the management of ladders, about which a book could be written.

In this example, Bell admires the sensitivity and engagement required in what is, for many, a day-to-day activity that may appear mundane or simple. For Bell, however, a proper management of ladders is a rural craft in itself – and tied up in this craft are the knowledge and skills passed down from one generation to the next. Bell understood and greatly valued those who worked with their hands – he certainly did not believe that 'book learning' was in any way superior, and there is a deep appreciation of such practical skills throughout his writing.

Bell exemplifies this in one of the most poignant passages in *Apple Acre*, which is of an ageing labourer called Tim Dukes. Dukes' particular skill is hedging, but he was then over seventy, and finding it increasingly difficult to get any work. Bell visits Dukes in his small cottage just after his wife has suffered a stroke. After offering him a glass of raspberry wine, Dukes takes Bell outside. Bell writes: 'He opened the door to his shed, and it was lined with implements, all the blades of husbandry: billhooks, reaphooks, slashers, blades of varying and subtle curves. All these tools were polished and greased; I should not think there was a speck of rust on one.'

Dukes wants Bell to see these tools because he wants him to appreciate them not only for what they are, but also for what they represent. Dukes is rightly proud of these tools because they represent a vocation, and as such are fundamental to his identity. As 'an expert hedger' they represent a way of life that is dependent on knowing the finer details of certain elements of nature. For Bell, 'that shed was a revelation after the rather haphazard room, and the ruinous state of the cottage. It was like a glimpse of culture.'

This culture is one that is grounded in traditional husbandry and a sensitive, close working of the land. It is a culture that is also born of a deep and lasting connection with the place in which one lives and works.

However, Bell shared with Dukes the sadness and sense of loss associated with the beautifully kept tools in front of him: although they were valued, they were increasingly without purpose and were becoming relics of the past. In his depiction of Dukes, Bell's purpose is not to offer an idealized vision of the life of a rural labourer, however much Dukes is admired for his specific skill. Bell sees him as a victim of modern farming practices that were becoming less reliant on the traditional knowledge and skills of rural craftsmen such as him.

Bell visits him again a little while later, after Dukes has succumbed to his own illness of old age, and he tells Bell: 'I've been worrying, that's the trouble. I can't help being worried, no pretending I can't.' Bell offers a stark portrayal of Dukes' reality – he and his wife, once active and independent, are no longer able to cope; Dukes dies soon after this visit. The importance of people such as Dukes to Bell in his life and writing should not be underestimated: Dukes serves a critical function in the narrative Bell constructs, as he is emblematic of the erosion of traditional husbandry.

Bell could see that as farming changed, so did the people and communities who were inextricably linked to it; Dukes symbolizes the craft and a rural culture that was being lost. Bell laments this loss, which is indicative of the husbandry he advocates: 'It was just a year ago I passed him cutting a roadside hedge. I think it was the last job he did. Going down that road yesterday I saw the cuts he had made, clean, no silvering, and thought of the greased hooks hung up, and Tim Dukes in his grave.'

This changing dynamic between people and the land can be seen in one of the last descriptions in the book, of a harvest festival. He depicts a rich scene in which the 'church itself seems to have quickened and flowered and fruited' as it is filled with the produce donated by local farmers. He likens the beauty and craftsmanship of the church's carving and stained-glass windows to the plentiful produce that came from the fields surrounding it. It is a moment Bell feels 'is the germ of all wholeness', in which 'there is enough meaning in the ordinary acts of country life to get the soul to heaven'.

However, Bell will not allow this vision of harmony between man, spirit and land to stand unchallenged, as he observes those who lay their precious produce in the church: 'Farmers' wives and daughters, although they produce all that is needed for a sturdy life, are often nowadays no better off than city folk for food, having town bread brought to them, commercial bacon in rashers, commercial flour.' Even at this traditional and significant festival, one that celebrates the labour of its community, Bell notes wider commercial concerns that were influencing rural communities such as these.

Thus, throughout the depictions and meditations in *Apple Acre*, Bell laments what is being lost in the name of technological and economic progress. However, in the final few pages of the book, he offers some hope that tradition – particularly traditional methods of husbandry – may one day come to be valued as much as technological progress. He makes the plea: 'Oh let men work in the light, in the air! It is not because we have exhausted the meaning of a simple life that we have discovered complexity.' He can see that World War II has, to a certain degree, helped the wider population of England rediscover this 'complexity' through straightened circumstances.

Bell further emphasizes the importance of valuing the 'meaning of simple life' as it is integral to England's identity, to its spirit: 'I can see these things beyond this war, clear suddenly through the incandescence; and I know it is not a dream or an escape, but an emergence. Here and there I come flashingly on the real England.' Fundamental to this is the valuing of skills, faith and community in which people will 'draw practical vision and integration for what they do'. For Bell, the catalyst for this vision and integration will not be found in a growing consumerist culture, but will only be achieved with a renewed appreciation for 'the power of the land'.

❦ ❦

Sunrise to Sunset was published in 1944 and is a semi-fictionalized account about the impact of World War II on Bell's family and on farming life. In the book he presents an account of farming more akin to when he started farming fourteen years earlier. Thus the skills and values of traditional husbandry, the importance of community, and Bell's expression of a natural theology are seams that run through *Sunrise to Sunset*.

Living close to the east coast of England as Bell did, there was a genuine threat of a German invasion of Suffolk, and children were evacuated to more inland rural areas during the early part of the war. As 'the sound of the guns from across the sea grew louder', and became continuous, it was becoming clear that Bell's wife and children should also be evacuated from Suffolk. Although the threat of a German invasion was growing, this was still a difficult decision for the Bell family to make:

> We vacillated all that weekend. We went to market: the square attitudes of the farmers reassured us. They had always stood in the street, talking. They went on talking, despite a bawling propaganda van imploring them not to give way to panic. They were talking of crops, of course, and the propaganda voice sounded much more panicky than they.

Despite the faith that Bell had in the farmers' unruffled and pragmatic demeanour – particularly in the face of the 'don't panic' declaration – they decided it was best to err on the side of caution, and Bell's wife and children moved for a time to a relative who farmed in Westmoreland. Thus, *Sunrise to Sunset* is unique in Bell's writing in that it is the only time he has written at length about an area away from his beloved Suffolk. It tells the story of his visits during this year, and his reflection on farming practices away from the land most familiar to him.

Indeed, it is clear from the opening few pages of *Sunrise to Sunset* that it was having pronounced effects on Bell, both geographically and emotionally: 'I crossed the Pennines. On the other side, the war seemed shut away. People were picnicking on the moors, lying in the sun with their coats off beside shiny cars. There were no barricades, no soldiers to be seen. It was like a dream after our Suffolk coastline.' Like many others, Bell feared for the safety of his family in Suffolk as the possibility of a German invasion increased. His journey away from East Anglia highlighted how far removed everyday life in East Anglia had become since the time of his rural trilogy.

When Bell was in Westmoreland visiting his wife Marjorie (or 'Nora' as she is called in his books) and his children, Anthea and Martin, he helped out on the farm they had been evacuated to – Brant's Farm. Bell soon became aware that farming such undulating land presented challenges unbeknown to him in the wide horizons of Suffolk: 'I began to have a sense of the hard labour involved in this Westmoreland farming [...] It looked an impossible country to farm; yet these folk farmed it and lived on it for generations.' Bell was struck not only with the topographical difference of this land, but also of the earth itself: 'I soon found myself hard at work on the "foreign" soil. It was grey and dusty with unaccustomed drought, and full of stones [...] it seemed as though nothing could live in it.'

Bell became aware that this steep and stony farm was like stepping back in time in relation to the husbandry of the land. Due to the inaccessibility of many of the fields, modern machinery could not be used, so many more traditional methods of farming remained. Bell writes that as a result: 'Everything almost was done by hand on Brant's Farm; and when you stood on the steep Brow, with the farmstead on your right, and little Beck Mill with its buildings laid out like a plan sheer below, you saw what was practically a self-contained organism.'

Bell was clearly struck by this vision of the farm as a 'self-contained organism'; it was a vision that resonated with his own view of farming practices. However, with the growing demand for 'efficiency' driven by new technologies and practices, he was seeing in his home county an increasingly significant movement away from this vision of husbandry. It is this tension – between the old and new orders of farming – that Bell examines in *Sunrise to Sunset*. In doing so, he sees that they appear to sit uncomfortably on Brant's Farm.

With John Rockfall, the farmer at Brant, Bell introduces a character who symbolizes the tension between tradition and technological progress: 'Rockfall hated machinery with a downright physical hatred [...] His stony tracks and bumpy fields were friendly to him till he tried to work a machine on them: then they became inimical. [...] He hated being a passive spectator of the machine, sitting on the seat.' Bell is not suggesting that Rockfall is a Luddite – quite the opposite. Rockfall knows his land better than any machine could know it, and resents anything that gets in the way of him working directly with it. Bell suggests that Rockfall has an active and close relationship with the land when he is farming – to use a machine is to become passive, and would serve to erode this relationship.

This sense of harmony between man and nature is further personified through Bell's description of the farmer herding his sheep on the high, isolated hills of Westmoreland: 'John Rockfall stood counting them, ruddy and shock-headed. Curiously old-fashioned and Quakerish he looked in his breeches, rough stockings and low-buckled clogs: in fact, the whole scene was elemental, allegorical, like a scene out of *Pilgrim's Progress*.'

This is farming at its most fundamental, in which man is at one with his subject and with his environment. By evoking this traditional pastoral scene – however much Bell may be romanticizing it – highlights that this relationship was subject to increasing strain. Bell was concerned with what is being lost as a consequence, with changing agricultural practices, and feared that men such as Rockfall, and their sympathetic husbandry of land and animals, were disappearing.

This concern is developed further by Bell when describing another traditional pastoral scene of hay being gathered by forks, horse and cart:

I was struck by the whole scene spread out before me. Rolling fields, ribbons of walls, woody thickets beside becks, white farmsteads; and then increasing bareness as the ground rose out of man's dominions to the solitude of the fells. The scene, expressive both of domesticity and eternal wildness, gave to the traditional work they were at down there the measure of a ceremony.

It is the balance between 'domesticity and eternal wildness' that Bell is struck with – to the point of reverence. The observation and exploration of this balance, likened almost to a ceremony, is a recurring theme not only in *Sunrise to Sunset*, but also in much of his later writing. In this, he is aware of the literary tradition in which he is writing and contributing to. Like many writers before him – from George Sturt, Thomas Hardy, George Eliot, Richard Jefferies, Thomas Bewick, John Clare, Oliver Goldsmith, More, all the way back to Virgil – Bell laments an old rural order – a happier age – that they see changing in their lifetime. In doing so, they look back to an earlier time in which men had a more harmonious relationship with Nature and with each other, creating pastoral vignettes that echo traditional practices and associated values. And, although Bell is not explicit about his faith, he is also suggesting in such vignettes a deep spirituality that runs through all things, connecting man and nature: a natural theology.

Another of Bell's recurring themes in *Sunrise to Sunset* is the fundamental importance of community. He appreciates this in Westmoreland when he describes his visit to Kendal market, where farmers from the local area came to sell their produce. He is struck with the interconnectedness of people and their surrounding environs, which is evident in the market:

> Even as the remote farmer, mounting his fell-top, was in view of the town, so here his wife was in actual touch with the inhabitants of that great view. A certain white dot of a farmstead would stand for the face and voice and animation of a neighbour. This is true community. Without actual contact, community is a sort of a broadcast myth.

The description of this market is an extension of the 'self-contained organism' of Brant's Farm: the people here have a clear and specific purpose, as they sell their 'produce of local earth' to the townsfolk. This is in sharp contrast to the market he describes at the end of *Men and the Fields*. It is, as Bell puts it, their 'settledness', which comes from living in and providing for their local community, that he values. To emphasize this, he contrasts them to the 'shifting, drifting, urban throng' of the consumers, and likens this contrast to a 'parable': each have their specific roles, but what binds them as a community is a sense of cooperation and interdependency.

Moreover, when describing the produce laid out on the tables, he once again values the balance he sees before him, a balance born of humankind's cooperative relationship with nature: 'What a medley; what a harmony. Hedgerow and brook and dairy – wading and plucking, and baking and churning. Upon the tables lay the essence of rugged acres and rugged homes, of a week of human energy in and about them.' At a time when an expanding war was devastating lives and communities across Europe, Bell portrays, in this description of the fruit of local labour, a deep appreciation of the interconnectedness and interdependence of man not only with nature, but also one with another. In doing so, he offers not only a lament, but also a hope.

Despite the portrayal of Rockfalls' farm practising more traditional, less mechanized ways of farming, it is clear that the broader changes in agricultural practices and markets were nevertheless beginning to have an influence on Brant's Farm. Bell describes Mrs Rockfall expressing her concern – over breakfast – about the changes in farming, in particular the structural support for farmers to produce more milk for the urban market. She notes that farming should focus on stock rearing and butter making, not milk producing, as it has a negative effect on the welfare of the cows in the short and long term. Milk that is being sold to keep the consumer happy comes at the expense of providing proper nutrition to the calves, which leads to less healthy and hardy cows. She can see that this consumer-driven strategy of milk production is not a sustainable or beneficial arrangement either for the farmer or for the livestock. Indeed, the words she spoke to Bell nearly eighty years ago in her Westmoreland farmhouse kitchen – 'But t'young things need mother's milk; and mine shall have it' – have not been heeded, and this has proved to be detrimental to us all.

What Bell sees in Westmorland echoes the concerns and hopes that are explored in *Apple Acre* and elsewhere in his writing: the importance of community, the relationship between man and his environment, and an appreciation of what is being lost in the name of technological and social developments. Because of this, Bell harboured a strong desire throughout the 1930s not simply to write about farming, but to live that way of life again. Biographer Ann Gander notes that:

> Times were changing, and farmers were eager to find ways to grow food more efficiently, and increasingly more artificially. Adrian felt that he would rather do things his way, embracing some of the new technology, but not yet abandoning the old methods if they worked best. To him, farming was a precious secret, a craft.

His time spent in Westmoreland with Rockfall practising more traditional methods of farming provided the impetus for him to turn his hand once again to his own husbandry, and in 1943 he acquired Brick Kiln Farm.

❀ 5 ❀

A PLEA FOR A RETURN
TO HUSBANDRY

THE RESURGENCE OF INTEREST in rural literature continued throughout World War II, with an increasingly wide readership appreciating the values Bell himself associated with the countryside. It was not only a place of provision and peace, it also strongly evoked English identity. This renewed interest in writing about the countryside meant that Bell's past and current writing found a new audience. *Apple Acre,* published in 1940, had sold 30,000 copies within the year, and *Corduroy* was being reprinted. In her biography of Bell, Ann Gander writes that his books 'were striking all the right chords in the hearts of those both at home and overseas. Letters were coming in from appreciative fans all over the world, on precious notepaper, on war-issue forms, even, poignantly, on prison note-paper.'

As well as all the soldiers who held dear their army-issued copies of *Corduroy,* evoking images of the land that they were fighting for, there is one letter that illustrates the importance of Bell's work to those separated from their homeland by World War II. It was written by Percy Kelly of the Royal Signals, who was based in Germany:

During long dreary months your writing came to me like a fresh breeze. So often have I been whisked away to an England of soft, peaceful meadows and changing skies – where the discovery of the first snowdrop would bring wonderment and joy … perhaps 'ere long

Potato Diggers

Image courtesy of Nicholas Holloway Fine Art, Private Collection

I will be sitting by my own fireside, stretching out my hand for *The Cherry Tree* – sincerely I could wish for nothing better.

However, this vision of rural England that contributed so significantly to the construction of English identity – of Englishness – was changing irrevocably as World War II came to an end, Matless writes: 'It was clear that the old ways had gone for good. Now a new order must emerge from the rubble of tradition. There would be no going back. Artificial insemination, mechanised labour and open-plan farmsteads were changing the face of the countryside and the fate of the countryman.' Therefore, however much farmers were being appreciated and supported financially during the war, Bell became increasingly concerned about the direction that farming was taking in England due to these changes.

In response to the development of government intervention in agriculture through numerous Acts in the 1930s, and then – more significantly – through the funding of a more mechanized and intensive approach during World War II, there was a growing desire amongst 'organicists' such as Bell to return to – or at least hold on to – older forms of agricultural practices. This desire was reflected in a growing number of publications that called for a return to more traditional methods of husbandry. Bell notes that 'it was the transformation of agriculture in war which gave organicism both urgency and coherence; the bulk of organicist literature was indeed issued in wartime.'

It was in H. J. Massingham's 1941 publication, from a symposium called 'England and the Farmer', that the organicists' concerns about the direction of agriculture were examined in more detail. This symposium brought together doctors, scientists, novelists and agriculturists to 'present a vision of an organic rural economy, polity, society and culture.' The majority of its contributors – with Bell amongst them as a writer and a farmer – would become founding members of a group calling itself the 'Kinship in Husbandry' in 1941. Central to this organic vision was a renewed appreciation and respect for the Earth itself. For Massingham 'there is a kind of music in the order of the universe, which penetrates man by and through the earth.... In losing touch with the organic processes of the earth, man is fouling the sources of his own being.'

In the light of this symposium, the 'Kinship in Husbandry' was formed and its members met during World War II. Its premise was, according to Bell, that 'man was plundering the earth's resources at a spendthrift rate and impoverishing posterity'. The meetings of this Kinship took place in Oxford and London, and sought to bring together people from different areas of life who had very similar concerns to discuss views on England's future. Members included the writer and poet Edmund Blunden, Lord Lymington, Hennell the artist, H. J. Massingham the rural philosopher, Lord Northbourne and Rolf Gardiner. Bell later notes that the emphasis of these meetings was …

> … on organic farming and living. We felt that a balanced life of people in an organic relationship to their home place was important. We envisaged not a divorce between industry and agriculture, so much as an integration of agriculture in what I now see was a too idealistic vision of the part-time husbandman, such as was the former village craftsman, who also kept a cow, owned a pasture and a patch of corn. […] Compost, of course, was a potent word among us: the utilisation of natural wastes.

Although the organicist vision had little policy or popular impact at the time, it does represent the foundation on which twenty-first-century 'Green' thinking is built. For example, good soil health, which in this view can only be achieved through organic means, was their primary concern. It was a concern shared by Eve Balfour in her significant 1943 study, *The Living Soil*, in which she argued that 'wherever the ecological balance of the soil is seriously disturbed, disorders in crops, animals and man follow.' This study, which was to become the founding document for The Soil Association (set up in 1945 with Balfour as its Chair) argued that soil was not simply a substance that held water and air together for crops to grow, it was instead, as Balfour notes, 'teeming with life. If this life is killed, the soil quite literally dies.'

Marjorie Bell c. 1935.

Adrian Bell and Margaret Batty c. 1934.

Adrian Bell c. 1970.

Marjorie Bell *c.* 1940.

Adrian Bell *c.* 1940.

Adrian Bell, 1918.

Bye Mill, Brant's Farm in *Sunrise to Sunset*.

Stephenson's Farm in *Silver Ley* and *The Cherry Tree*.

Adrian Bell, Stephanie Bell and Francis Bell with parents, *c.* 1925.

Adrian Bell and Marjorie in the late 1960s.

George Hempstead (Bell's first employee) on the binder.

Marjorie and Adrian Bell with the artist John Nash, 1934.

Bell at work on Brick Kiln Farm with Elmore Sayer and Bill Porter, *c.* 1948.

Robert Bell.

Fanny Bell.

Seabrooks in *Silver Ley* and *The Cherry Tree*.

Adrian Bell helping on Blenkharm's Farm (*Sunrise to Sunset*).

Adrian Bell with 'Bob', 1923.

Drift Cottage in *The Cherry Tree*.

Balfour considers that modern methods of farming – predominantly the use of artificial fertilizers – are in opposition to the care that soil requires for it to remain alive. As a consequence, there is also a moral and political dimension to her argument – she attests that we have a duty as individuals and as a society to care for the earth: 'You may ask, what have all these platitudes to do with humus? The answer is, a lot. Our attitude to the soil is dependent on our attitude to life in general […] The vegetable kingdom has for too long been considered a sort of factory.'

Therefore, Balfour, Massingham, Bell and others wanted to counter what they saw as a growing exploitation of the land through the steady industrialization of farming practices. Their increasing concern for the health of the soil arose not only because of the impact that increasing mechanization and artificial interventions were having on it: it was also informed by recent research and publications, with Albert Howard's *The Agricultural Testament* (1940) being particularly influential. Howard, a botanist and organic farming pioneer, focused on nature and the management of soil fertility by organic means, primarily through composting. Although Bell did not throw his heart and soul into the Kinship in Husbandry (according to his daughter Anthea, he was particularly wary of its primary founding member, Rolf Gardiner, and his pro-German views at the time), the focus on a close relationship with place, and on utilizing all natural resources in a sustainable way, was very much shared by Bell.

Bell notes that 'such was the mood of the times' that in the week of the inception of the Kinship in Husbandry, the exposition of its ideas received over half a leader page in *The Observer*. As noted, however, the values of traditional husbandry that were shared and espoused by the Kinship members were not being taken into consideration by farming policy makers. Farmers who ran organic, mixed and rotated farms were increasingly forced by the War Agricultural Committee, and latterly by Ministry of Agriculture policy, to sacrifice the diversity enabled by pasture land and to plough it up in favour of more intensive food production and money crops. Government subsidies were readily available to do this, a process that gathered pace throughout World War II.

It is worth illustrating the huge impact this had with reference to the government's Ministry of Information 1945 review, *Land at War*, on the agricultural war effort. Matless notes that 'images of conflict and pastoral are brought together' in the publication, and in doing so 'harness the cultural power of county tradition, yet suggesting that its landscape needed shaking up'. In the review, the author writes: 'When in 1939 we turned again to the land, we found it no more prepared for war than we were ourselves, with [...] crumbling barns, weedy fields, and depopulation...a general apathy.' However, it was given massive impetus by *The National Farm Survey of 1941–43* (styled as a second *Domesday Book*), which classified all land in relation to its management and potential productivity. By 1945, 6,500,000 acres had been ploughed up in the drive to turn farming into a modern industry.

Although the increased status and financial resources awarded to farmers was welcome, the drive to turn it into a modern industry was a very concerning one for many. In 1945 Philip Mairot, in an essay called 'Self Sufficiency' in the collection entitled *The Natural Order*, described the increasing preoccupation with mechanization a 'technocratic fallacy'. He saw that a 'period of mounting technological triumph had begun to affect the minds and souls of men, for they are unable to resist the idea that scientific fabrication is the only cultural idea of the present and the future.' When considering the recent development in modern agricultural practices, Mairot issued a stark warning:

> We have unleashed forces that are subversive of all natural order. It is perhaps something to discover, as we are doing, that in the social life of man, politics are a higher category of thought than economics – that in the long run, politics determines economics, and not vice versa: but we have yet to realize fully that both are determined by culture, and that it is our culture which has suffered a distortion. In the correction of that distortion one of the first necessities will be the right understanding of agriculture – and especially our own.

This subversion of the natural order, in which economics dominated ideology and policy in relation to the land, led to traditional farmers making way for the business farmer – and in so doing, changed the culture of farming itself. Philip Oyler, in his 1945 article 'Feeding Ourselves', again taken from *The Natural Order*, argues that husbandry should be regarded as the most important occupation, and is concerned that 'those who look upon the land as a source of money making will exploit it sooner or later, and will fail to cultivate or plant for posterity'. Instead, Oyler stresses that 'it is a real love of the land that is needed first, for where the land is loved, it will be treated with the care and respect it deserves, and good crops will result automatically.'

However, this love of the land proved not to be the primary concern in progressive agriculture, and as we have seen, there were many who did not subscribe to this vision. In *Mechanisation and the Land*, published in 1945, C. Henry Warren questions the wisdom of replacing skilled hand labour:

> The land of this country, and in fact every country, cries out for more of the living on the land – more men, more animals, and increased output per acre in quality. [...] The greater the concentration of machines, the greater must be the dilution of men on the farms, and with this a lesser degree of tactual contact with the soil and the life on it [...] If the future criteria of agricultural efficiency are to be cheapness and output per man; if first principles and natural laws are to be ignored, as they must be to capture this variety of efficiency; if the power-machine is to be the principal means to this end, then it will need no uncommon powers of perception to forecast the disastrous result.

In Warren's view, it is only through 'more of the living on the land' that a love and care for it can be achieved, which is the opposite of what was happening before. Therefore the increasing mechanization of farming, together with the introduction of government subsidies, was to an extent at odds with the higher regard that the general public had for farming as a result of their efforts to increase food production during World War

II. Indeed, writing in 1946, the rural writer and ecology pioneer John Stewart Collis dryly observes that 'The reading public is so accustomed these days to hear praise of the countryman – the swing in this direction taking place before the war broke out – that it is almost a shock to find that this is not yet realised by country labourers themselves.' Although the public's appreciation of those who worked the land may have been more widely forthcoming, it had little impact on the fact that more and more people were leaving farming, as new technologies meant that their labour was no longer deemed necessary. The 'drift from the land' of agricultural workers between the two world wars (approximately 10,000 per year) would continue as farms embraced industrialized methods of farming.

In this context, it is perhaps not surprising that Bell's next work of non-fiction, *The Budding Morrow* (1946), is more philosophical than any of his previous work. In addressing some of the concerns raised by Oyler, Warren, Collis and others, he develops his discussion from previous publications, particularly *Apple Acre*, questioning the direction that modern agriculture was taking – increasing centralization in policy-making, a widening separation of experience from theory, the importance of maintaining diversity in the Countryside, an increasing domination of the land, and a continuing disconnection between the country and the city. The majority of this book was written near the end of World War II, when, despite the optimism that peace would inevitably bring, the food shortages in Britain and in many parts of the world were as acute as they had been at any point during the war. In many ways it can be viewed as Bell's manifesto for farming in post-war England.

In *The Budding Morrow*, Bell once again draws upon his experiences as a farmer working his own land. Therefore the book opens, as many of his do, with a description of an early morning. On this occasion it is 6am on a cold January day, and Bell appears to be in a philosophical mood as he plans the farming day ahead: 'As I sit milking, I consider the day's work. Work on a farm is not just a thing you do: it is something that you are: it is part of yourself. And altogether it is good.' As Bell has done previously, he presents a sense of oneness with his work in which farming is integral to his identity. For him, the two cannot be separated; as he puts it: 'Farming is a vocation, it is a way of life and it is engrossing: it is a "many-thinged thing", and my task is legion.'

But Bell appears to go further than he has done in earlier writing when he proposes what he believes farming can offer the individual beyond the farm and its fields. He attests: 'Wisdom there is to be had in farming, I do know that. By its practical-sentient approach you can assess other trades, professions, assertions, researches, politics and passions.' For Bell, the 'severe bodily and mental discipline of farming' means that it engages both the body and the mind in the day-to-day affairs of the earth. As a consequence of such an engagement, he believes that farming can offer one a powerful position to 'achieve a just estimate of many a question of the hour – the decay of faith, machinery versus humanity, science versus religion. I do not know how this is so; but in the light of agricultural experience you can read the Gospels, St Paul, History, Philosophy, Poetry anew.' Farming is not simply a practical activity for Bell: it requires deeper emotional engagement in order to respect and care for the land and animals.

As a result of this holistic approach, in which reason and feeling is equally important for sympathetic husbandry, he believes that other activities can be measured against farming. Unlike many 'academic' professions, he feels that to be able to assess the human condition with authenticity, both your body and your mind need to be engaged in a clear and worthwhile purpose. Without this, any consideration becomes a purely theoretical one, uninformed by what he sees as the fundamental experience that agriculture provides: 'Above all, tutored by frost on the fingers, by the hand grown numb cutting kale for this warm feast of cows, by the vision of the seed also, the goodly seed that dies into life that Christ spoke hard fact, literal to daily living in all times.'

Although it rarely comes to the fore in his writing, Bell had a degree of religious faith. But it is not this that he is articulating in this increasingly impassioned passage from the opening pages of *The Budding Morrow*. Rather, it is the general principle that people – those with faith or those without, but devoid of any experience of working with the elements of nature – make judgements in a vacuum. Bell is critical of those whose generalizations and moral proclamations are based on ignorance rather than experience:

> One comes to resent the self-imposed public moralist who 'interprets' that teaching in the light of modern conditions, making it an excuse for condoning a number of things which we know to be not in the true and kindly grain of living; to whip up antagonisms in Tom, Dick and Harry which they do not naturally feel, by identifying other people, whole nations, with abstractions, and calling them collectively the Evil Thing, the Power of Darkness, and so forth.

Bell suggests that the prejudicial propaganda that these 'self-imposed public moralists' propound, leads to separation and conflict. Bell's plea, which sets the tone for *The Budding Morrow*, is made because he strongly believes that humankind's growing detachment with his environment is a prime reason for man setting himself against man – physically, emotionally and spiritually. In a passage that contains both humour and gravitas, Bell undercuts those who pontificate without practical experience:

> This sounds all right in a radio sermon; but after you have all week been wrestling with the problems of the earth, you realise that it won't do. The Power of Darkness is not so obligingly metaphorical at six a.m. in January, but it is a fact that hits you hard between the eyes when you grope for the shovel in the turnip shed and collide with the handle of a chaff-cutter.

The lack of connection with the land, and any practical relationship with it, leads to an abstraction of authentic experience, which can lead to difference and separation. For Bell, it is the earth and humankind's reliance on it that binds humanity together – when this is lost sight of, division and prejudice fill the void. The abstraction of authentic experience that leads to this separation is a growing concern in Bell's later writing.

This concern becomes even more pressing in *The Budding Morrow*, and is first raised when Bell recounts a talk he has with a friend who is an expert in keeping cows: 'In my friend's opinion there is no doubt that the constitution of stock in the country is declining owing to milk forcing.' Increased desire for milk from a growing urban population was driving intensification such as this in rural communities. Bell could see that it was placing demands on the land that would not be sustainable in the long term: 'This whole problem of milk-selling is a serious one – how to dovetail it into a thorough, soil-enriching husbandry.'

This is just one example from a wider economic and political context that was forcing huge changes in farming practices. World War II, and the push for rural (and urban) communities to 'dig for victory', meant that land needed to be as productive as it possibly could be. Bell recounts the call to arms made by the Minister of Agriculture in 1940 for all to play their part in this:

> The Minister of Agriculture has just broadcast an appeal for volunteers on the land, and has emphasised the seriousness of the food situation. For sugar and potatoes Britain must rely entirely on her own land, and for other foods – meat, milk and bread – on her own resources to a greater degree than ever before. This is on the eve of victory in war. Our fight, then, is still on. [...] Here surely is something new in farming, as I remember it; even in wartime farming: the aim being service before profit.

As a consequence, new scientific, technological and mechanical advances that would increase productivity should be utilized by all farmers: indeed, it was their duty to their country to ensure they did so. The War Agricultural Committee, who ensured that all available and suitable land was put into production in the nation's drive for self-sufficiency, closely monitored that farmers were availing themselves of all the new practices opening up to them. But this new 'arable culture' that was being promoted and funded by the government was at odds with the 'old' view of farming. In this old view, Bell notes, there was 'an appreciation of a limited amount of wilderness, so the old-fashioned farmer loved his plantations almost as much as his ploughed fields; he preserved their wildness'.

The farmer did this because he knew it was the right thing to do in order to maintain a diverse range of plants and species. However, Bell was realising that these old ways could not survive for long with the rise of new agricultural practices. He understood that he was farming in an era fuelled by the centralized support of the War Agricultural Committee, in which 'big wages and big machines, prices and purchasing power' were becoming more and more influential in the farming of the countryside. As a result, he could see that farming in sympathy with the land – 'a quality husbandry' – was becoming more challenging because it was not seen as a priority by those who were driving these developments.

Bell was not a traditionalist for the sake of it, though; he could see the value of some technological developments, and, as he writes, was happy to embrace progress when it served him better in his day-to-day running of the farm:

> Now I have occasion to live with, and use, and love both the old and the new. My daily life is a constant mingling of the two. One day I am ploughing with horses, another with a tractor. A hurricane lantern serves me in one place, an electric switch in another. Oak beams and pantiles, sheet iron and concrete. The age is transitional: that is reflected in the daily life on less than a hundred acres.

Nevertheless the nature of this transition, which would gain further momentum as a result of the 1947 Agriculture Act and the increasing involvement of outside businesses chasing the financial rewards of farmers' subsidies, began to trouble Bell more and more. He could see the influence these changes were having on farming practices, and with them the significant impact on the countryside and those who worked it. As a result, a pronounced tension between progress and tradition became more evident in Bell's work. Although he can see the benefit of new methods of farming, he does not accept that the old ones should be swept away as a result.

For example, when harrowing and digging ditches to improve the topsoil and drainage of the subsoil of one of his fields, he describes discovering a former drainage system that was over a hundred years old: 'In the interval, nobody had drained so closely, nor scoured the ditches to the bottom, for no one who has worked on this farm knew of these pipes. They are a skeleton of a former husbandry.' Those who farmed this field in past times knew exactly how best to work with the land to best benefit it, and so themselves. It is such traditions of husbandry that should be looked to, learnt from and valued.

But it was not only the environment and traditional husbandry that would be compromised by the increasing capitalization of the countryside: it was the ability of farmers to make a living. If an increasingly competitive and open market dictated prices for produce, then it would be the producers who would suffer. As Bell considered the Minister of Agriculture's call for more food production, he also considered those soldiers who might wish to do their duty in this cause once they had returned from war:

> What is the hope of ex-servicemen wishing to take up agriculture? Marketing, marketing, and again marketing. Let the price of every kind of farm produce be assured: let it be known for several months ahead: let it be based on weight and quality, and the ex-servicemen can have confidence in making a life for himself and his family on the land. All his powers can be concentrated on learning his job of farming, and not on trying to hold his own against a horde of dealers, those vultures of the so-called 'open market'.

If, as Bell here argues, achieving 'a quality husbandry' was becoming harder in an increasingly capitalized farming 'industry' in which the 'vultures' of the 'open market' held power over the producers, this meant that over time the identity of those who worked the land was also being challenged: because of the nature of their interactions with the land and with each other they would need to adapt in order to survive and continue farming. When considering similar concerns in post-war American agriculture, Wendell Berry (author of *The Unsettling of America: Culture and Agriculture* (1977)) observes:

> And this community-killing agriculture, with its monomania of bigness, is not primarily the work of farmers […] it is the work of institutions of agriculture: the university experts, the bureaucrats and the 'agribusinessmen', who have promoted so-called efficiency at the expense of community (and of real efficiency), and quantity at the expense of quality.

The impact of agencies whose primary concern is production and profit has had a fundamental influence on those who farmed the land prior to their arrival. Because they have changed the identity of farming, they have also changed the identity of farmers themselves. Bell could see this happening, and the reader can see throughout his writing how this identity is constructed through an individual's interaction with the land he works. Therefore, Bell is keenly interested in how the environment influences and shapes those who work closely with it to make them who they are:

> Sturt writes about the old farm worker loving his tools; and how the shapes of them and the memories cling to them, and along with his dilapidated cottage, make up that sense of 'home' which is the only comfort in his old age – his whole 'philosophy' in fact.

When contemplating this in relation to the move towards mechanization on the farm, Bell wonders 'if this be true of scythe and spade, may it ever come to be true of a tractor?' Bell questions whether the intimacy that is achieved through a physical relationship with these tools and their connection with the land can be achieved when effectively once removed from it. Part of the issue that Bell has with mechanization is that with it comes a greater ability for man to control and dominate the natural world, rather than work with it, as he sees we should do:

> We talk of winter relaxing its grip. But the grip of spring is much more compelling. It is high tension. I must control something much more complicated than the most complex switchboard. I must be aware at the very pores, if I am going to farm well. And this tension corresponds to the tension in all growing things. I am tuned in – if you like – to the same wave-length, and being so, am more aware – vitally aware – of the spring. It is not only the vision of process, but the process in action in myself. Thereby work ceases to be work; it becomes will to effect, and the body the merest tool.

Thus Bell suggests that this idea of intimacy is born of the simple but fundamental belief that man is part of the natural world, not separate from it. For him, farming is a correspondence with the natural world, in which he views the process not from a point of dominance, but from a point of acute self-awareness of how he needs to interact with it: 'Process in action in myself.' In these terms it is akin to a spiritual engagement with the land, in which work 'becomes will to effect, and the body the merest tool.'

For Bell, this close connection is inevitable – and necessary – if man is to work in balance with nature, rather than against it, when he states that 'Man in nature, exercising homely wisdom therein, and modifying the scene, imposes a growing order. Not a monotonous one.' In this, man and nature enhance each other and are drawn closer together, and the qualities of each contribute to their identities – thus he concludes by suggesting that: 'A tilled landscape is like an open book, in which you can read not only of nature but of human nature. Pass a man's field daily and you know that man.' For Bell, anything that undermined this close connection with the land was detrimental to the land, and to those who worked it.

This challenge to individual, rural and, for many, to national identity – or sense of Englishness – that resulted from rapidly changing agricultural practices and demographics during the 1940s and 1950s also contributed to the increasing separation of the country and the city. Although a tension between the town and its rural environs has always existed, Bell could see this tension increasing. For the first time in his writing there is an explicit expression, in *The Budding Morrow*, of the frustration he feels about the way rural communities are regarded by their urban neighbours. He writes that: 'England has no signpost to Nirvana. What a very good thing for us all it would be if the country scene ceased to be used simply as a sedative, a sort of aspirin to the urban constitution.'

The idea of the rural idyll – an English Nirvana – runs deep in the English psyche, fostered and mediated through centuries of artistic and literary constructions. It is a construction of which Bell is highly critical, for it is not based on any understanding of the reality of rural life. He sees the 'poetry' of farming as 'an illusion of urban minds', which only results in fuelling misunderstanding and ignorance, and in forging a greater divide between the country and the city. Warming to this theme, Bell challenges the common stereotype that persists regarding the rural worker as lacking in relation to the urban one. He adds:

> Compared to the modern farmer, the townsman is slow, insensitive, and lulled to the expectation of automatic reactions in all he touches. Yet advertising persists in presenting scenes of indolence and rose-bowered incompetence as 'farming', in order to lesson sales-resistance. Old men astride old horses gossiping for ever outside old inns; farmers leaning over gates; joy-of-harvest pictures of as many people poking about on one stack as would staff 200 acres.

As well as accepting and perpetuating a marketed, aesthetically pleasing vision of the countryside, to Bell, the townsman had also become so disengaged with his natural environment that he was becoming 'slow', 'insensitive' and 'unthinking' in his interactions with the outside world. The countryside had become something separate from the important aspects of life – it was seen more as a place of recreation rather than as having a practical impact; it had become an idealized vision of England.

And it is this disregard – or ignorance – of the reality of rural life which so frustrated Bell:

> And then, when farmers call for new equipment, and a plentiful supply of water, light and building materials, they are accused of uglifying, exploiting, destroying the spirit of the land. What of the rats that scurry round the old barn, and the snow that sifts down on the corn through the pretty pantiles? Waste is not lovely.

From his own experience as a farmer, Bell knew that for rural communities to survive, they must be valued by all the country's citizens. It must be realized and appreciated that the countryside is not simply to be conceptualized and regarded as some ancient 'spirit of the land'. Yes, the countryside – or rather the 'landscape' – is a fundamental part of English identity, but it should not be preserved for the aesthetic pleasure of urban day trippers and holiday makers: it is a practical, changing place that needs investment and support. In this, Bell believed that 'the spirit of the land' would only remain in an environment that could provide improved conditions and resources for farmers. However, having farmed through a period when, economically, cities were prioritized over farming communities, he witnessed the struggles faced by the latter:

> The country-bred youth looks round, and what does he see? Almost every cottage in his village a condemned cottage; officially condemned way back in the thirties. No new houses, no light, and water in buckets from the pond. Why should he stay?

This neglect was brought into sharper focus when the government – and a predominantly urban population – looked to those who worked the land to sustain them in a time of war. Farmers, and those who relied on them for their own livelihoods, were at long last benefiting from some financial investment. Along with this, many contemporary observers, such as Bell, hoped that a greater appreciation and understanding of rural communities would also follow, and that the increasing cultural and economic division between the country and the city would be reversed. If this were not achieved, and investment in the countryside were not maintained, as happened after World War I, Bell was concerned for the future of these rural communities:

> Who, then, would work the land? New people, out of love with the motives of their urban fathers. In love with labour and new tackle, giving and enduring. In love with the edged tool of action, living the seasons. Drawing vigour from vision, its only true source. A great and tangled hedge of English country character and practice is before them, lovely in its wildness, but thorny with prejudice. With reverent but scientific blade they set to work on it. It is a re-civilization they are engaged in.

He does, nevertheless, have hope that people – 'new people' – whether country bred or town bred, will once again seek to re-establish their relationship with the land. In this hope, they will come to realize that the 'motives of their urban fathers' leads to an unfulfilling existence because they have become separated from nature and from purposeful labour as a consequence. Instead of a continuing drift from the land, Bell hopes that people will once again appreciate the tradition and the values of the 'great and tangled hedge of English country character', and return to them. For him, this reconnection with the land and those who have worked in, and cared for it over generations, would result in a re-establishing of what is important in life: community and sustainability. This is why he describes such a process as a 're-civilization', and a 're-establishing' of a sense of Englishness.

However, Bell understood that in the increasingly capitalist culture of the twentieth century, people were encouraged to consume rather than create, which for him is the opposite of re-civilization. Bell considered that being ostensibly a consumer in a consumerist society was an unfulfilling way of life, and he was hopeful that others would come to a similar realization. He quickly learnt that farming is a process of creation, a process that connects individuals to something more than themselves. He is not suggesting that everyone should return to the land, but he is saying that in order to create an English countryside that is anywhere near approaching the nostalgic, idealized vision commonly portrayed, and on which English identity is founded, our rural communities must be as thriving as our urban ones:

> When you see once more the farm garden as well tended as its fields, and not a place of fallen trees, broken hen-coops and old iron; when once more a homely grace reigns in the farmhouse parlour, and not a cold clutter of tasteless furniture; then by these signs you will know that agriculture is again what it was and essentially must be – the basis of all culture.

Bell's belief 'that agriculture is the basis of all culture' is more fully articulated in the chapter of *The Budding Morrow* entitled 'Pure Drinking and Clear Thinking'. After musing on the recently built school area, and the purpose and relevance of its academic pursuits ('this building looks like a first-rate instrument of modern civilisation'), he offers another reason why a sympathetic connection with the natural world is so important to our wellbeing. He picks up on the idea noted earlier that people will 'fall out of love with the motives of their urban fathers' because 'muscular and mental inertness will become intolerable to them, as it is to some who have already come through to a feeling that is driving them out of town life and town pleasures.' His view of the negative effects of town life and town pleasures is unequivocal: 'Muscular slackness is the root of all evil, which a hundred small daily indulgences make formidable in aggregate. The remedy for lassitude is hard work.' For Bell, an engagement with purposeful, practical activity is hugely important, as he sees it as a creative, not consumptive exercise.

The idea that people in towns live a life that is too passive for both body and soul is explored further with his consideration of what he sees as a 'soporific spell over the old'. In this, he shares Berry's view that: 'We must learn again to think of human energy, our energy, not as something to be saved, but as something to be used and to be enjoyed

127

in use.' With traditional husbandry being replaced with 'progressive' farming methods, less labour was required on the land. This meant that not only were more and more people being forced to find work in the towns and cities, those who were left on the land were less closely connected to it.

This process of geographic and practical removal from the land was also becoming a cultural and emotional one. Again, Bell emphasizes the vital importance of man being engaged in, and having an investment in, the work that he does. In this, he shares a view expressed by George Stapledon, a grassland scientist and environmentalist, in his 1943 book *The Way of the Land*:

> For a man to work without some feeling towards the material he handles, without pride in the accomplished task, no matter how trivial, and without interest in the final results of his toil, is one of the greatest tragedies that can come upon a human being. To work without interest or any feeling of love is to be denied the enjoyment of perhaps the greatest pleasure this life has to offer, and in the fact that such a high proportion of the workers of the world are denied, or deny themselves, this pleasure is to be found one of the chief causes of widespread social neurosis.

For Bell, this fundamental investment and enjoyment – a 'feeling of love' – in what one does on a daily basis creates a culture in which individuals and communities can thrive. If this sense of purpose and achievement is lacking and it becomes merely a financial transaction between the employer and the employee, any sense of pride is undermined and a supportive culture is difficult to achieve.

Instead, what Bell saw was an increasing brutality in modern methods of farming which, over time, would fragment and dissolve rural culture built up over generations, and damage the land these farmers were supposed to be custodians of. Although the extent of the social, economic and environmental impacts of these modern methods would not become apparent until the latter half of the twentieth century, he feared the effect of agriculture becoming further mechanized, specialized and intensified through the increasing influence of outside agricultural business interests. These included tractor and machinery manufacturers and pesticide and fertilizer companies. He understood that farming would inevitably change, but he was seeking a balance between traditional methods of husbandry and those that were being proposed by the government and business alike as progressive:

> If we really believe in modern machinery paving the way to an enrich-
> ment of personal life, let us now use it with soul averted to things of
> yesteryear. We still talk of putting our hands to the plough. Would it
> not be better to bestow our spiritual enthusiasm on our actual daily
> life?

In this view, Bell felt that if developments in farming methods were to benefit those who adopted them, whilst not negatively impacting the land on which they were practised, we would have to adopt a more forward-looking attitude in order to achieve such harmony – what he calls 'a natural association'. In this, he does not believe that the methods of British Victorian industrialism, which were becoming increasingly influential and damaging in agriculture, were the answer. Instead, he thought we needed to consider the methods of those 'untainted' by this heritage, and for this he looked towards Scandinavia:

> To them, modern power on the land does not mean large-scale indus-
> trial farming, on the contrary. Nor in building does it mean gimcrack
> bungalows. They, if anybody, can make something of it that is calm
> and sane: happy, lovely: convert it to the service of posterity, family
> and home.

In looking towards the predominant ideology in agriculture at this time in Scandinavia, he saw a vision for farming that combined modern methods with the values and practices of traditional husbandry – particularly the importance of keeping labour on the land.

Consequently, he believed that agriculture could progress in a different way from the one he was currently seeing in England. He believed that farming practices could change, and effectively incorporate some modern technologies, but he stressed that the well-being of the land, together with the people who work it, had to remain a priority. Bell questioned whether this would actually be the case, and had serious doubts as to whether a more sensitive relationship between the two would evolve. The concern that industry would dominate 'the quality of old husbandry' was not on the agenda of policy makers, for it 'represents an idea that our rulers cannot yet stomach: an equal partnership between industry and agriculture'. A more natural association between the old and the new should be at the heart of the interaction.

Therefore, Bell presents in *The Budding Morrow* the possible long-term consequences of an increasing mechanization and intensification of agriculture. He could see that these methods went hand in hand with the growing emphasis placed – primarily by bureaucrats and business interests – on 'efficiency': 'But to-day, we must be more concerned with efficiency in farming, even to the point of making it an ethic, simply for the fact that there are so many people in the world to feed; a largely devastated world, a largely office-based world.' Bell was acutely aware of the imbalance that existed between those who produce, and those who consume. This fundamental imbalance was driving a move away from traditional methods of farming towards what was viewed by many as more efficient methods – methods that embraced the capitalization of the countryside.

Of course, the need for greater self-sufficiency as a result of World War II had played a significant part in instigating this change. In such a context, if all those who need feeding are to be fed, then 'efficiency' must be embraced as a moral obligation, irrespective of whether it is the right thing to do for the long-term welfare of the land and its people. Bell could see why a drive for efficiency was necessary, but foresaw the negative impact that such a drive could have. Instead of the land being something man endeavoured to work with, and to look after – to husband – it would become a place in which man and machine would seek to dominate. The cumulative effect of this desire for 'efficiency in farming' is arguably worse than Bell imagined: it has resulted in hugely powerful agribusinesses and supermarkets, and continues to fragment rural communities, and be disastrous for the environment.

Thus with such an agricultural ideology beginning to dominate, Bell also stresses in *The Budding Morrow* the importance of maintaining diversity, something which is often compromised in any drive for efficiency. He depicts this diversity in practice when describing a visit to a friend's farm:

Watching the hay climbing the elevator in his stackyard, and thinking of the crops I have seen – the peas, runner beans, onions and corn-flowers, as well as the barley and sugar-beet – it seemed that he had removed the rigid boundary between farm and garden. [...] The point of this is that my friend is a successful farmer, and makes as much profit per acre as any man. Diversity pays, as he manages it – corn and flowers and vegetables. I should guess his farm returns more per acre than the alternate sugar-beet and barley in huge blocks, which is another form of modern farming, with its liability to disease. His farm is founded on pigs; the other on yearly and increasing doses of chemical fertilizer.

The diversity that Bell observes is in contrast to the view of farming that dominated at the end of World War II. He could see that maintaining variety was not seen as a priority by those who sought to employ modern, progressive practices, and who had the primary aim of making farming more efficient and productive. Bell shares Balfour's chief concern – that is, for the long-term well-being of that which sustains all of us – soil. If this is to be achieved, Bell understands that more traditional mixed agricultural practices must be maintained when he writes that 'Variety is the salt of man's life, and of the life of the soil. As long as we stick to variety we have nothing to fear from mechanisation.'

However, in farming communities that were being more and more influenced by the interests of outside businesses, diversity was something that was being lost, and this would have a significant impact on the 'life of the soil'. Once again, Berry shares Bell's concerns when considering the state of farming in America in the late 1970s. He foresaw that a trend towards industrial agriculture would inevitably lead to it being run by corporations rather than by individual farmers. And he feared the consequences if this proved to be the case:

> The cost of this corporate totalitarianism in energy, land and social disruption will be enormous. It will lead to the exhaustion of farm-land and farm culture. Husbandry will become an extractive industry; because maintenance will entirely give way to production, the fertility of the soil will become a limited, unrenewable resource like coal or oil.

The traditional method of keeping soil in a healthy condition is through crop rotation. This keeps disease in the crops to a minimum, whilst manure is used in order to replenish nutrients and increase the hummus layer that is a vital element of a healthy soil. However, the methods of husbandry Bell admires and values were being challenged, with artificial fertilizers leading the way. Unlike today, there was little evidence at the time that artificial fertilizers would damage the soil. However, Bell was nevertheless sceptical of its use: 'I have no case against synthetic ferti-liser, but every time I look at a bag of that stuff the words "No residual values" pass through my head.' By residual values, he means that however much artificial fertiliser a farmer may apply to his crop, none will carry over until the next year; Bell wonders where the unused chemicals end up. He, like many farmers, struggled with the idea that, unlike the tried and tested manure, 'that stuff' would improve – or even maintain – the quality of their soil.

They perhaps acknowledged the short-term benefit of artificial fertilizers, but questioned the long-term effect that they might have on the land and its surrounding areas. For them, there is no sustainable substitute to manure. This traditional method of using waste from the farm to enrich the land surrounding it has been practised for thousands of years, and many farmers at this time were sceptical that such a simple and effective method of both waste disposal and crop preparation could be improved upon by companies whose primary purpose was to make money.

Nevertheless, that does not mean that they did not try. In one rather humorous passage in *The Budding Morrow*, Bell describes a farmers' club meeting where a representative from a fertilizer manufacturer endeavours to persuade those present that the traditional method of fertilizing the soil with farmyard manure was inadequate, suggesting that it was often excessive in nitrogen and deficient in phosphate. In his role as a fertilizer salesman, he goes even further when he tells the assembled that the 'making of muck is the most uneconomic job on the farm'. The idea that manure production is regarded as 'uneconomic' is almost laughable – it is the best fertilizer for the long-term health and structure of the soil, and a free resource most farms produce. Indeed, with the increasing popularity of artificial fertilizers, many farmers started buying in these fertilizers for their farms – but then they were also having to pay to get their 'muck' taken away.

This illustrates the growing influence that business was having on farming communities. This influence had huge practical implications for the farmer and his land, and also contributed towards the changing discourse in farming and its relationship within its own communities and with the wider urban population. The growing influence of chemical companies, seed companies and farm machinery companies encouraged farmers to become consumers as well as producers: they had to have these products if they were to become effective in their farming 'methods'. In doing so, it was changing the culture of farming in its practices and beliefs, and also in name: agriculture was becoming agribusiness.

In a time when, driven by such business influences, farmers were encouraged to specialize, Bell again stresses the importance of variety in maintaining an agriculture that benefits the land and those who worked on it: 'Man must have bread and roses: farm, garden, factory, social exchange. Life must be various, and the variety must fall into a pattern.' He was anxious about the trend for specializing because it would ultimately change a culture to the long-term detriment of it. Man can only have 'bread and roses' if diversity in all things is valued and sustained.

And with such diversity comes a sense of balance that must be strived for. Balance between man and nature, between labour and profit, between man and machine. Bell was certainly very sceptical of the growing mechanization and specialism he could see taking place in farming, but he was aware that traditional and modern methods could co-exist for the benefit of all. He suggests that a balance between the two is needed if farming is to benefit from past and current knowledge and skills: 'In my experience, sometimes the Laboratory is right, occasionally Medieval England is right. The two might combine to produce real wisdom.'

However, he could see that a balance between them that could perhaps lead to 'real wisdom' was not easily achieved: 'But Medieval England is locked, bolted and barred into his Certainty, while to the Laboratory mind the very lilt of his sayings is as suspect to the smell as incense to a Puritan.' He couldn't see why traditional methods were not valued more highly, and he also didn't see why progress could not provide huge benefits to the traditionalist: 'Perhaps the farm worker will become a small yeoman again, his own master, by virtue of the machine. In that case, the machine would not enslave, but set free.' Consequently, like many farmers at the time, Bell could see at once the advantages and disadvantages associated with modern, so-called progressive farming methods.

As Bell considers what the future might hold for farmers after the war, he speculates that it will be a competitive one for them, with consumers wanting their produce as cheap as possible. For this to be achieved, further and more rapid intensification would be inevitable:

> That means machinery. But what machinery? How much? Machinery is still largely experimental; and there comes a point, fairly soon reached on a smallish farm, when the cure is as bad as the complaint: i.e. over capitalisation is as bad as the heavy wages bill. The same labour must produce more food; that is the basis of reorganisation.

The English farmer would find himself in an increasingly global market in which he would be competing against imports of food that were less expensive due to subsidies and lower labour costs. As a result, the only way to reduce his own cost would be through such intensification, and, as time would tell, economies of scale: smaller farms would not be able to survive this capitalization of farming. At this point in his writing, Bell is struggling to reconcile this movement towards intensification and mechanization with what he believes is best for the land and its communities. However, towards the end of *The Budding Morrow*, Bell endeavours to avoid offering a polarized view:

> Well, there it is. I must stop saying this is good and that is bad. I know nothing. I have two horses and a tractor [...] I have a wagon that is one hundred years old and a tractor-trailer that is one year old: these bring in a harvest of sheaves that are almost as old as time. I use superphosphate and a limited amount of synthetic nitrogen, but I turn all my straw into farmyard manure with cows and bullocks [...] All these things, ancient and modern, are married into the work of the farm. I use them equally, and with an equal mind. If you ask me which is best, I cannot tell you. It is easy to lay down the law, to take up an attitude – horse power or mechanisation. You may notice some apparent contradictions in this story of our transitional farming of today. If that is so, it is because one appreciates the good points of whatever one is at the moment using. To say outright, this is beautiful and good; that is ugly and bad, would be too slick for truth [...] it all depends on human nature.

Although Bell is taking a pragmatic approach here, he nevertheless questions what society is gaining from removing labour from the fields and placing it in factories: 'I sometimes wonder whether the labour spent on producing and perfecting machinery to do the work of the fields is not as great as that which would be spent on doing it by hand as in the past.' However, he readily acknowledges that his view is biased, as he would rather be in the open air than in an industrial building, and appreciates that many prefer the more controlled urban environment.

However, what concerns him more is who actually benefits from it: 'When I visualize tractors coming off the conveyor belt, and the mechanics in attendance, I feel I am an exploiter of sweated labour.' In the organization of labour that capitalism demands, it is the factory owner, the big business, who avails himself of the 'sweated labour' of others the most. He also sees the growing lack of connection between labour and its deeper rewards of pride and independence: it becomes a purely monetary relationship in which those who manage the labour benefit the most from it. 'The fruits of our labours' is an idea that becomes a misnomer in such a social and economic context. For Bell, however, it is a fundamental one to appreciate if people are not to feel disempowered within society.

At the end of *The Budding Morrow*, Bell makes clear what he had implied before in his observations of how farming was developing. One of the criticisms he makes explicit is the effect that the encroaching influence of big business and bureaucratic intervention is having on those who seek to make an independent living:

> The common man is feeling for a common denominator of Good, which autocrats, big and petty, fear and seek to frustrate [...] It is impossible to be the architect of one's life any more, or of one's own farm, without constant reference to the concept of social conscience rising like a green tree through the broken tablets of man-made law.

Bell considers that a move to centralized policy making, which increasingly favours larger-scale farming and more industrial methods of practice, will inevitably mean that small-scale farmers will not be able to survive independently of these mechanisms. He questions whether such changes make for good farming, although to a certain extent he can see the positives in so far as farmers now have the tool power 'to master the land, and dodge the weather' as never before. But he sees this very much in the context of necessity born of the need to feed a population during the challenges of World War II, and does not see this as either desirable or sustainable in the long term: 'Is it life? As I see it, it is coping with an emergency.'

He understood the need for pragmatism in embracing new technologies if it meant increased productivity in the short term, but warned against the impact this would ultimately have on the nature of agriculture and those involved in it: 'Being myself a commercial farmer (who isn't) I still affirm against all the agricultural "realists" that farming *is* a way of life.'

For him, farming embodies the qualities that were being eroded in an increasingly capitalist and divided society. Bell believes that having a close working relationship with the land can narrow this division, stating that 'daily, in all acts of farming, I have found food for thought about these things. The basis is, that satisfaction comes not of looking at life, but of living it, achieving something with it.' Creativity, which is a fundamental characteristic of farming, should be valued in whatever we choose to do with our lives.

However, Bell saw a society that was increasingly encouraged to become consumers and observers rather than producers. Such a cultural shift worried him, not least because it would hasten the dislocation between man and the natural world; a dislocation that would be detrimental to both. For Bell, farming is so much more than a business or even a vocation. As he explores in depth in his next publication, *The Flower and the Wheel*, farming is synonymous with natural theology: it is part of human nature. It also embodies that which makes a worthwhile life: a symbiotic connection with the land, and with the communities in which the individual works.

Plough Horses

Image courtesy of Nicholas Holloway Fine Art, Private Collection

❧ 6 ❧

THE QUIET REVOLUTION:
THE CAPITALIZATION OF THE COUNTRYSIDE

GOVERNMENT INVOLVEMENT IN FARMING was cemented with the 1947 Agricultural Act, and changed farming practices in Britain irrevocably. It guaranteed prices for farmers' produce and provided security for tenant farmers and their tenures. It also had the effect of capitalizing agriculture beyond any previous levels, speeding up intensification and mechanization. Industrial agriculture, in its infancy in the 1930s, grew rapidly throughout the 1940s and 1950s with the support of this Act. The impact that post-war subsidies had on traditional farming communities and on the countryside has been profound. In his book *The Killing of the Countryside*, Graham Harvey argues that the negative impact industrial agriculture has had on these communities and on the environment is a direct result of the government's subsidy policy, which made diverse farming on a small-scale level very difficult:

> At the start of the last war there were almost half a million farms in Britain, including part-time holdings. The majority were small, mixed units of less than 50 acres. [...] Before the age of state protection farmers needed to grow a range of products for financial security. [...] At the same time, almost a million workers were employed on British farms. [...] Yet it cost the taxpayers nothing [...] If politicians had truly understood agriculture they would have recognised that the mixed farm structure was a national treasure to be nurtured and prized.

In *A Planning Survey of Herefordshire,* published in 1946, the official attitude that Harvey identifies of these post-war agriculture policy makers is evidently clear. One of the survey's recommendations was to get rid of farms and smallholdings of less than twenty acres, which accounted for 40 per cent of the farms in Herefordshire. They were regarded in the report as 'uneconomic units'. Other recommendations included clearing orchards because they were 'hopelessly intermixed', and increasing mechanization and new techniques ('an industrial plan').

This focus on industrial farming resulted in a significant change in the size of farm that was seen in the post-war English countryside. There were 226,000 small farmers (each with fewer that fifty acres) in England and Wales in 1938, the year before government intervention in farming. Thirty years later, this number had dropped by a quarter. In contrast, during the same period there was a 40 per cent increase in farmers with more than 300 acres, whilst the price of farmland itself rose by nearly 90 per cent. The impact of big business was clear.

As we have seen, Bell was certainly not alone in observing that 'progressive' farming was having significant negative impacts on the land and its people. In *The Natural Order* (subtitled *The Return to Husbandry*) – published in 1945 – Bell's essay, 'The Small Farm', was one of a number of others from farmers and writers (including Massingham, Blunden, Gardiner, the Earl of Portsmouth) who were becoming increasingly concerned with modern, more 'industrial' methods of farming. A number of these figures were also, to varying degrees, associated with the Kinship in Husbandry mentioned in the previous chapter.

Before commenting on Bell's contribution to *The Natural Order,* it is worth considering Massingham's introduction to it in a little depth because – perhaps more than any other rural writer contemporary to Bell – his views on agriculture and society illuminate those that Bell presented in the two texts explored in this chapter: his essay 'The Small Farm', and one of his most significant books, *The Flower and the Wheel.*

In the introduction to *The Natural Order,* Massingham outlines the agricultural picture in 1945: 'Monopoly spreads like flood-water over individual businesses and undertakings. [...] Centralization and large-scale semi-totalitarian planning have already reached lengths that would have stupefied our forefathers, and worse is to come.' Similarly to the concerns expressed by Bell in *The Budding Morrow*, he stresses that there is a crucial need for a reconsideration of recent developments in farming. In doing so, he is critical of the way in which an individual's freedom is being eroded through the growing influence of larger institutions, whose primary purpose is to make money: 'The vulgarity of commercialism is omnipresent,' Massingham argues. 'Local self-government is vanishing under our eyes, and the liberty of the person is in pressing danger.'

He could see that such 'centralisation and large-scale semi-totalitarian planning' helped create a cultural and economic climate which ensured that the interests of businesses could flourish. This was often done with the misguided notion that what must be good for the economy must be good for the country as a whole. Instead, then – as now – it simply led to the monopoly of big business, leeching power, choice and freedom away from the individual.

If this trend was to be reversed, Massingham believed that one of the first areas that needed to be addressed was the growing industrialization and commercialization of agriculture, and a restoration of agricultural self-sufficiency. In this, he shared C. H. Gardiner's view when sounding a note of caution about the long-term effects of 'big money' coming into farming, because he feels that outside business concerns will inevitably come to dominate the practices in the countryside and put profitability above all else. Massingham writes: 'I fear that we hear too much about a "prosperous" agriculture after the war. It is an adjective I mistrust [...] I would prefer that reference was made to a *healthy* agriculture.'

Therefore, in challenging the increasingly dominant practices of modern farming, Massingham, like Bell, advocated a return to husbandry. In doing so he was quick to emphasize that this has nothing to do with reversion to a past regarded as old-fashioned and obsolete. Instead, such a return is, Massingham suggests, 'a means of recovering a certain order and mode of being which is timeless and universal, which is, in fact, part of man's nature.' However, this does not simply mean farmers returning to a more traditional, less intensive and mechanized method of working the land. In addition to a change in farming methods, there needed to be a change in ethos, away from a centralized economy that inevitably centralized wealth and power. And so, together with the other contributors to *The Natural Order*, his vision was not just related to agricultural practices but to society in a broader sense. This vision, Massingham notes, included:

> The proper balance of town and country, the full development of the home market, agriculture the *only* primary industry, the abandonment of the idiocy of long-distance farming by urban clerks and officials who try and cheat nature with their own little industrial gadgets, the recovery of the country of its indispensable self-government, and thereby the recovery of local and personal responsibility – these are all contained in the term 'husbandry'.

Both Bell and Massingham appreciated that husbandry depends on an intimate knowledge of the land being worked – it cannot be done by proxy. Consequently, inherent in effective husbandry – something that would benefit both the countryside and the wider population – is a greater focus on the local picture, rather than the national one. If, rather than concentrating predominately on the economic wellbeing and growth of urban populations, there was a greater emphasis on fostering healthy local communities founded on traditional agriculture, then a more balanced relationship between the populations of town and country could be fostered.

Moreover, in rejecting methods of farming that aim to 'cheat nature', Massingham is also seeking a more balanced relationship with nature itself. If farming of the land is dictated from afar – from people and business whose vested interests are separated from the earth that is worked – then it likely leads to the exploitation of this land. Thus, integral to a more locally focused ethos, is a return to a fundamentally organic approach to agriculture in which the priority is to protect the mechanics, the chemistry and the biology of the soil. He notes that such an ecological approach has been the one taken for thousands of years before rural society felt industrial influence. Massingham, like Bell, is unequivocal in stating that this is an approach we must return to. 'Cultivating the soil' Massingham states 'is the first and most important of all civilized activities because the life of society depends upon it.'

In this, he sees husbandry not simply as a practical, economic or environmental issue, but shares Bell's view that it is also an ethical one. For both, the priority of agriculture must be to maintain the health of the soil, otherwise all else will fail – it should not be a matter of economic choice, it is a moral issue. Bell also considers that it is only through such careful husbandry that we will be able to sustain our needs with the resources we have. As Bell attests, modern methods of farming will not be a long-term solution because they do not operate in sympathy with the land:

> Large-scale industrial farming is by its very nature extensive, and will fail simply because it has not the capacity to produce enough food per acre. Only enough men on the land skilled in the arts of husbandry can produce enough food to safeguard the nation against a world shortage of food. This will not be a scarcity artificially induced by the modern economic system, but a real one. A return to husbandry is a double wisdom, that of right values, but also of self-preservation.

Consequently, it is clear that a common view in *The Natural Order* is that our relationship with nature, and in particular with the fundamental element of it, the soil, needs to once again become a closer, more physical one.

In his own contribution to the collection of essays, *The Small Farm*, Bell develops this idea. He argues that it is only through a skilled husbandry that a more sustainable model for future agriculture can be achieved, rather than through what he calls 'large-scale industrial farming'. In suggesting this, he is wary of how this can be achieved with a greater reliance on machinery. In the essay, he argues that there is a greater harmony between the farmer and his land on smaller farms because they have not yet significantly substituted day-to-day practical tasks with technology. Although Bell had reservations about the economic sense of small farmers investing in farm machinery that might be used only once a year, he can also appreciate the benefit of mechanization so long as it is employed with the judiciousness and sensitivity that only a small farmer can have with a thoughtful understanding of his land: 'a semi-mechanized small farm is not an uneconomic unit to-day.'

However, he is concerned that a balance between traditional and modern methods of working the land should be maintained, stating that 'A fully mechanized farm is uneconomic, whether it be of fifty acres, or five hundred or five thousand [...] The small farmer is more likely to use discrimination in the use of the machine, which is essential to good soil texture and good economy.' For example, he states that a farmer who farms seventy acres is more likely to know each one of his fields intimately than one who farms 7,000, thus he knows how to manage the working of them for the long-term health of their soil. Because Bell understands that agriculture's economic productivity is entirely dependent on the health of its most important element, the soil, he also understands that the use of machinery on this precious resource can be damaging to it if not managed with care and close attention.

Like Massingham, he cannot understand how a large farm that is becoming increasingly mechanized can be as productive, or as economically efficient, as a smaller farm that uses machinery in sympathy with the land. As Massingham makes clear in his introduction, the only way this can be achieved is through a return to, and maintenance of, the small farm: for him, it is 'the keystone of husbandry'. Integral to this is that men 'skilled in the arts of husbandry' must be valued more than any business model of farming, or any machine that is deemed necessary to implement it.

Bell also counters the dominant narrative of the advocates of progressive farming by suggesting that large-scale industrial farming will ultimately fail because it cannot produce enough food. His view was echoed over seventy years later by Professor Herren in the aforementioned *World Agricultural Report*, which concluded that 'industrial crop growing would not feed the world. It was unfit for purpose.' Both Bell and Herren propose the benefits of smaller scale farming, and challenge the notion that it cannot meet the demands of a growing population. In doing so, they both highlight the fact that, although more labour intensive, production per acre can be increased if mixed farming methods are adopted.

Bell illustrates this when he notes that the average size of a farm in England in 1944 was less than one hundred acres, but questions whether these should be amalgamated to suit 'modern conditions'. His argument against such amalgamations is that farmers on smaller holdings are able to focus on the 'right values' – in other words, they are more likely to offer skilled husbandry. For example, small farms encourage mixed farming: dairy, pasture, cereal, root crops and livestock. The variety on these farms benefits both the fertility of the land and the health of the animals. Bell also warns against large-scale or small-scale farms trying to approximate industrial models, because, unlike these models, farming is uniquely subject to the 'vagaries of weather and crop flexibility'. Because of this, farming needs to be adaptable, and smaller farms are more capable of such adaptability.

Bell recognizes in this essay, as he has done elsewhere, that the rise of capitalist consumerism and larger farms was practically, emotionally and spiritually separating people from the land. He cannot see the benefit of a consumer culture that encourages a removal from the basic resources that we all rely on. He writes: 'It is just this physical awareness that life of the radio car-owning standard mesmerizes away. These accessories have become the central, incessant fact. At all costs, we must get back to physical experience, and mend the poverty of our resources.' Central to this 'physical awareness' is the fundamental rejection of the 'ideal which views man as a consumer only, and forgets that he is equally a producer.' He sees the developing culture of consumer capitalism captivating – 'mesmorizing' – increasing numbers of people, which lessens their ability and desire to engage creatively with their environment.

Bell develops his criticism of this ideal that man becomes a passive consumer:

The high peak of the consumer's universe: the Riviera *rentier* liverishly sucking in the products of an exploited world while creating and producing nothing, and only able to continue to live at all by constant colonic lavage ... while it is true that man works to satisfy his hunger, it is equally true that man satisfies his hunger in order to be able to work.

In this stern critique, Bell offers a vision of a society that is decadent and almost parasitical. It is a society that prioritizes the individual over community, and leisure over work. He was starting to see that work was no longer a way of life for people, instead people were working to have a 'lifestyle'. For Bell, traditional farming was a creative act, and as such the antithesis of consumerism.

Consequently, a quarter of a century later, when he reflects upon the concerns he had for England's future immediately after the end of World War II, he maintained that, wherever possible, we must endeavour to get back to a 'physical experience' in relation to the land and to our work. The environmental benefits of organic farming and living were becoming clearer with every passing year when contrasted with the impact the expanding use of pesticides was having on wildlife, bees, agricultural animals and humans. Indeed, it was only fifteen years after World War II that Rachael Carson's hugely significant book, *Silent Spring*, was published, which starkly highlighted the extent of this impact to a wider audience.

Bell, like Carson, advocates the importance of maintaining a close relationship with the land as well as the people directly around you. Sympathetic environmental and community engagement was fundamental to Bell's way of life: he, along with others such as Massingham and latterly Wendell Berry, the prolific American novelist, poet, environmental activist, cultural critic and farmer, believed such engagement should be fundamental to everybody's way of life. The vision that Bell had been formulating throughout World War II, and had communicated to a certain extent in previous publications, came to a fuller, more polemical philosophy in his next publication, *The Flower and the Wheel*.

❀ ❀

The Flower and the Wheel was Bell's first book to be written and published after the end of World War II. In it, he develops in greater detail
the themes that he explored in *The Budding Morrow* and in his essay 'The
Small Farm' – in particular the harmony that should be sought between
old and new methods of farming for the benefit of both the land and the
rural communities that work closely with it. In *The Flower and the Wheel*
Bell writes of 'the need for a return to the patient earth', and in the sleeve
notes to the 1949 Bodley Head edition of the book it is noted that: '"Back
to the land" is no empty catch-phrase for him, but a burning philosophy,
a way of life, based on the universal truth of man's dependence on the soil
for his sustenance.'

In terms of communicating this 'burning philosophy', Bell is more
direct and detailed than he has been in any of his previous publications.
There is a greater consideration of the changing nature of agriculture in
Britain, and a greater concern as to the long-term consequences of these
changes. However, it is also a hopeful book – it suggests that we can
reconcile tradition and progression in farming, and make it a sustainable
way of life. If *The Budding Morrow* outlines Bell's practical manifesto
for the future of farming in England, then *The Flower and the Wheel*
presents a philosophical one.

In H. J. Massingham's book, *The Faith of a Fieldsman*, written in 1951,
he pays close attention to *The Flower and the Wheel* in a chapter called
'A Litany of Earth'. Bell is a writer whose work he knows well, and he
suggests that this book is the best he has published so far. He argues
that Bell has made a departure in form from his previous work (perhaps
with the exception of *Apple Acre*), in that there appears to be very little
narrative, noting that 'it just bubbles up here and there'. Instead, he
regards it as a book of meditations:

> The book is divided into short chapters, often starting off or bursting
> out from some quite casual encounter or trifling incident in the daily
> farm and home, and there is no more beginning and end to them than

a piece of cloth cut into lengths by the tailor. In fact, there is no form, no structure, build-up, sequence, evolution in the book at all. It is the most extempore book an author could write: it hovers, drifts, tacks, veers like a yacht caught in uncertain breezes, or Ariel letting himself go after Prospero had released him.

In regarding *The Flower and the Wheel* as a book of vision, he draws comparisons to *Centuries of Meditations*, written by Thomas Traherne, a seventeenth-century Herefordshire rector. Both books, Massingham argues, have the 'texture of thought, quality of vision and intensity of perception [that exult] in the transfiguration of the common appearances of earthly life. [Bell's] book is utterly remote from the industrial mentality, and illumined with a light independent of time.'

Bell was approaching fifty years of age, so perhaps not surprisingly this subtle and perceptive appreciation of nature, and of humankind's place in it, is more pronounced in *The Flower and the Wheel* than in his earlier work. For example, consider Bell's beautifully observed description of plum blossom, writing of its beauty and its transience – the 'spirit of spring':

> We should be aware of what we miss. A few moments of such chance encounter with the spirit of spring should overwhelm us with our physical loss. For here are not moments and colours, but the touching on a new, constant intensity. There should be a new discernment, a new sympathy between man and woman, and between man and man, matching this new delicacy of life.

There is an acute awareness of the preciousness of time, and with its hurried passing there is an appreciation that growth will inevitably lead to decay, and that decay will inevitably lead to growth. This 'constant intensity' is the nature of things. And there is a hope that with such appreciation we should pay closer attention to one other. In a world so recently torn apart by war, new relationships needed to be forged, and communities, both large and small, needed to be rebuilt. If this 'new discernment' were to be achieved, then Bell writes that we should be instructed by nature, as this is where balance and harmony can be found:

> Life presented itself in all simplicity – full sun, cool breeze, green corn and a singing sky. The surge of wheat to the horizon was not a monotony; it was a unison [...] At my feet was an answering variety of the minute: wild flowers of the field verge bordering the wheat, and insects running to and fro among them. One could not be but thankful, sitting there: thankful for everything, for nothing.

It is through such a contemplation of nature that we become one with it, and the self becomes unimportant. For Bell, his relationship with the natural world approaches a meditative one, becoming a balm for his soul. In a great deal of his earlier writing he presents a predominantly practical view of his natural surroundings, which is to be expected as he gets to grips with farming it. Alongside this, he depicts moments of aesthetic appreciation in his admiration for the land he works. However, it is only in his later works – as he passes middle age – that he offers such a spiritual view of the countryside, something akin to a natural theology. He believed that the further man moved away from having a symbiotic relationship with nature, the worse it would be for him.

Bell recognizes that if we are to reconnect with our natural environment, then integral to this 'new discernment' must be how modern practices and ideologies can be married to more traditional ones. For example, in the opening chapter, entitled 'Beginning Again', Bell begins with a description of a newly painted white windmill turning on Saxted Green – a village he is passing through on a journey in rural Suffolk. He is struck with the aesthetic beauty of this white windmill on a village green, along with what it evokes and symbolizes. It conjures up images from his childhood and early farming life, and is also part of an earlier tradition that was fundamental to our existence: the 'necessity of our daily bread' as he calls it. However, he undercuts a nostalgic vision and brings us sharply into the present when noting the juxtaposition between the old and the new: 'To complete any picture of Saxted Green I must add that a line of great metallic pylons cuts right across it, handing the curving wires from each to each, from distance to distance.'

As he presents these objects of times past and times present together, Bell does not pass judgement – he is simply appreciating the huge significance of their function in our existence: 'I found in them, as in nothing else, a sense that matched the turning of the mill.' What Bell is appreciating here, and is seeking elsewhere, is that there should be a closer fusion – and perhaps balance – between tradition and modernity.

However, as he witnessed the massive changes that were taking place in the countryside due to the rise of industrial agriculture, he feared that important skills and values were being lost in this march of progress. Bell believed that we needed to consider more carefully how those in the pursuit of progress could embrace traditional knowledge and understanding for the benefit of a greater number of people, not just economically, but also spiritually. He extends his discussion from previous works, writing that there needs to be a greater synergy between technological advancements and traditional methods:

Form and feeling somehow, somewhen, must be reborn. These are a necessity that will not wait – the daily bread, the very breath. [...] We shall make silly things, saurians, grotesques, at first. Look at our tractors [...] Unwieldy groaning monsters of mental creation, pictures of a man's mind trying to take a different course.

In *The Flower and Wheel*, Bell offers some direction for this different course. In doing so, he does not want tradition disregarded or dismissed in the manner he sees happening in the practices of modern farming all around him. Instead, he wants a closer relationship between the past, the present and the future in order that a greater harmony between the old and the new can be achieved. He is hopeful that if this is realized, then: 'Eventually we may reach again, at quite a different level, beauty, charity, even the anarchy of love.' Bell remains optimistic for the future, but this is founded upon a thoughtful appreciation of humankind's relationship with the land, and with each other. If this relationship is to be appreciated, and a reconnection with the land achieved, then the past cannot be swept away in the name of progress.

Therefore, Bell could see that the continuing mechanization and intensification of farming after World War II brought with it both appreciation and disquiet to those who worked with the land. Bell appreciated that jobs that were previously hugely labour intensive were completed more quickly and with significantly less struggle: 'What pains our forefathers took to plough in a certain way [...] Hard labour, painstaking carefulness without end. Now a young man sitting up there on a padded leather seat is curing this field, and along with him ride holiday children, one holding a bouquet of cowslips.' Bell's contrasting depiction between endless 'painstaking carefulness', and the comfort of a tractor driver presented as though it is in a parade – with children and flowers – is a deliberately striking one. Here, progress is presented in positive terms, and Bell regards the employment of the tractor as a 'great good'.

Indeed, Bell further emphasizes the challenges that his forefathers have faced between the two world wars, in which, in his view, 'Farming retrogressed centuries'. In doing so, he directly addresses the idealized vision – a vision predominantly created and perpetuated through the culture of an urban population – of those who have worked the land for centuries. He is under no illusion about how difficult it has been for others before him when he writes:

Books have been written on the manner of life that our forefathers led on their medieval holdings, and painters have pictured the idyllic days of swains with innumerable angel-faced infants under roofs of mouldering thatch. But the real thing could be seen here and there about the country, even in the twentieth century, and it was far from lovely. [...] He was a serf in everything but name. Such was the lot of a small farmer on stubborn soil in the years of neglected English agriculture.

In acknowledging past rural challenges, he viewed the modern developments in farming practices as a positive force for change. The 'power of the tractor gave him new mastery' over his land, and offered the possibility that, finally, farmers could make a living from it without the struggles of their ancestors. Although the evidence in the fields around him was beginning to suggest otherwise, he did acknowledge in *The Flower and the Wheel* that perhaps new methods of farming need not inevitably lead to an increasing dominance of the land – a relationship that Bell fundamentally disagreed with. If man dominates, then he fails to understand that which he seeks to control – thus leading to a growing separation. Although Bell did not necessarily regard mechanization as incompatible with good husbandry, he did see there was a danger that it could easily become so.

Therefore, Bell understood that if a more responsible use of modern farming methods were to be achieved, then we needed to examine our own relationship with the technology associated with it. In the following extract, at the end of Chapter One, Bell evokes a moment in which he is forced to reflect upon his own relationship with the changing nature of farming. Once again, he uses the most significant symbol of this progress – the tractor – to do this: 'One morning I came to the spot where the tractor stood warming up for the day's work. No one was beside it. The singing of the birds and the breeze died from my ears as the throb of the tractor invaded them.' Isolating the tractor from its driver enables him to view it differently and away from its primary function of serving man. At first, he resents the impact it has on his own relationship with his natural surroundings, but once he becomes accustomed to the 'throb of the tractor' he begins to see a deeper connection with it:

I saw that machine anew. I saw not a machine, but a pattern of the human mind. This thing is an idea, a piece of brain stuff. But there is something more to it than that. I watched the radiator fan revolving to the regular beat of the engine. So many revolutions to the minute. So many revolutions to the month, to the year, to the century. Revolutions of the earth, of the sun and the stars; complex, mathematically exact, from the timing of the moon's orbit to the structure of a honey-cell.

152

It is here that Bell sees the tractor as an act of creation, almost like any other. Rather than it being something artificial – something man-made – it is regarded as something that is part of the natural world, not separated from it. The beat of its engine is the heartbeat of a living thing, whilst the revolution of its fan is linked at once to cosmic and earthly creation. In this moment, the tractor, the earth and the stars become one; the separation between them dissolves in an almost metaphysical vision.

Any division is challenged further by Bell with the arrival of the driver carrying a freshly picked primrose: 'He laid the flower on the tractor. The flower shook, lying on the body of the machine. The flower of life lying within the law of the wheel. The flower of our life also.' For Bell, the laying of the flower on the tractor humanizes the machine, and reinforces its connection to the natural world. And, like placing flowers on a coffin or a grave, it is also a mark of respect for the objects on which they are laid. It is this description, this vision, that provides the inspiration for the focus of *The Flower and the Wheel*. It is a hope that tradition and progress can co-exist, that harmony between old and new methods of farming can be achieved for the benefit of the land, and for its people.

Although Bell wanted people to foster a closer relationship with nature, and seek a more harmonious balance between traditional husbandry and progressive farming methods, he had, as previously noted, serious doubts that it was heading in this direction. Indeed, in Chapter Five he makes explicit the concerns he has for modern society, and in doing so offers a number of reasons why nature should not be regarded as something 'other' to the supposedly important concerns of an increasingly urban culture. Firstly, he turns his attention to the education system that he believes is doing the younger generation a disservice, and writes:

> In our so-called education we substitute written notes for memory – notes are dissected bones, memory is alive, imaginative. We cram the youth with facts and figures, and take away from the man the one thing needful for his manhood, the power to be alone with himself in nature.

Bell believed that if we prioritize knowledge over creativity (in this system of education he regards them as mutually exclusive), then we will produce a population that is unable to think for itself and adapt, particularly in a rural environment. In this, he is questioning the value of an education that is geared primarily toward preparing students to meet the demands of jobs that are being created to serve an urban economy.

The problem he sees with this is three-fold. Firstly, despite the government's drive to increase production in light of World War II, the general education of Britain's post-war generation was very much focused away from the skills needed to do this with sensitivity to the environment and the rural population. The rhetoric and the money may have been positive for the farming community, but the education on offer did not match this. Intentional or otherwise, the message was clear: farmers and rural workers were still regarded as having a lower status than their urban counterparts, who needed to be 'educated' to do their jobs. To compound this, the growing reliance on mechanization and associated technologies meant that as older farmers left the land, the skills of traditional husbandry were being lost.

In a time of significant government investment in order to increase production, the loss of traditional husbandry was not lamented by the plethora of businesses who saw the financial opportunities in marketing 'modern and progressive' methods of farming. But such a loss would lead to a style of farming that would become increasingly specialized, as diversity does not suit a business model. Not only would this have a huge impact on the environment, with farmland turned into monocultures, it would also have a huge impact on the culture of the rural population. Generation after generation of farmers have passed down methods of farming that served the land well, and which served them well, too, although often not in financial terms. They used this inherited knowledge and the skills honed from years of experience of working closely with the land, to work with it, to husband it. However, with the massive and swift changes in farming taking place, Bell called for a greater integration of the old and the new:

Our real danger would be if we were to forsake our local genius, and sacrifice quality in an attempt to compete at a lower level in cheapness and mass production […] I am not saying we have all to be hand-crafts-men working in an old-world atmosphere. Hand and machine can be allied in the ideal of quality, just as in agriculture horse and tractor are allied, not necessarily antithetical.

As he suggested in *The Budding Morrow*, Bell is once again advocating a renewal of rural culture. For Bell, it is this 'local genius' that underpins rural culture. It is a mixture of skills, knowledge, experience and, above all, pride in the work that is undertaken. And so, rather than seek to replace it, technology should be utilized to enhance more traditional approaches to farming. Whilst modern techniques may save the farmer significant labour costs, they are often rather crude in their application, and can undermine the qualities inherent in more traditional husbandry. This is why Bell wanted them to be used in sympathy with the land, rather than being used – as he could see was increasingly happening – to dominate it.

Therefore, this distancing from the land has huge significance both for the land and our relationship with it, because it leads to losing a sense of place. In an increasingly mobile country, in which more and more people had no direct connection to a specific place because they were commuting or moving to cities for work, Bell highlights the importance of maintaining a deep understanding of the places in which we live, and the positive effect this understanding will have upon us. Thus he writes:

If we knew our own place we should have wisdom. Because to know a place is to become aware of a peculiar essence, a quality. And that peculiar quality goes deeper than mere knowledge: it is the various genius of Britain. It is more than a sense, it is a power. The power passed into the people, into their minds and into their hands.

In these last two extracts from *The Flower and the Wheel*, Bell stresses the need to have a fundamental respect for where you live. However,

155

with modern farming methods encouraging a dominance of the land, together with people increasingly working away from where they lived, having a sense of place was not only becoming less important, it was also becoming less achievable. Having this sense of place, which brings with it 'wisdom' and a 'peculiar essence, a quality', means that people are more likely to be engaged with their local environment and their local communities.

For Bell, such engagement with 'place' leads to empowerment and responsibility, which is good for the land and for the individual. However, in changing economic and social contexts immediately after World War II, this engagement with locality was becoming significantly harder to achieve. Not only were greater numbers of people moving away from rural communities to urban areas, but these urban areas also had a greater influence in rural communities due to businesses seeing opportunities to capitalize on 'progressive' farming methods.

Although Bell remains hopeful that a more sustainable agriculture may be achieved through a renewed appreciation of locality and traditional husbandry, he once again acknowledges that preconceptions associated with the countryside must be addressed. For example, it was previously noted that Bell took issue with Hardy's aestheticized depiction of a man and horse harrowing in the field, and that, during his first year as a farmer, he was soon discovering that the reality of working the land was far removed from the Hardy portrait. In *The Flower and the Wheel*, Bell once more counters traditional – and persistent – literary representations of those who work the land. This time it is Wordsworth's reflections that he challenges:

> Wordsworth was once troubled by a misgiving: 'Say there were not always someone to plough and sow and reap for me, while I walk with Nature?' A fundamental question requiring a frank answer. I read on: he meets a poor old leech-gatherer; then shelves the whole problem with a moralizing laugh.

Although Wordsworth's intention is to demonstrate an appreciation of

those who 'plough and sow and reap', for Bell it is a superficial and damaging one because it perpetuates an opposition between the producer
and the consumer. Therefore, those who work the land are seen primarily as figures who are separate from writers like himself, who 'walk
with Nature': separate culturally, intellectually and socially. Implicit in
many such literary portrayals of the countryside and its people is that of
hierarchy, illustrated above with what Bell interprets as Wordsworth's
'moralizing laugh'. There is a clear sense that those who work the land
are viewed by an increasingly dominant urban culture in less favourable
terms than those who have moved away to lead a life in the cities.

Thus, as Bell notes, this raises 'a fundamental question' about the
relationship between the country and the city. Indeed, what Wordsworth
suggests concerns him: that is, those who produce the essentials of life
are not regarded and valued in society. Instead, farmers are more likely
to be viewed as mere providers to a more important, 'better' educated
urban population. And it is this separation of those who produce and
those who consume which Bell is grappling with. He sees at first hand
not only a movement away from the countryside to the city, but also
a growing division within rural communities. In both cases, it is the
growing consumerist culture that is driving this fragmentation of rural
society. However, in a rather hopeful view, he does not believe that
this can last because he does not foresee industrialism – that which is
driving 'progressive' farming methods – as having a long-term future.
He writes:

To toil in commercial factories is not the Englishman's destiny.
Industrialism is dying – cracking and tottering, rather, for it never
lived. The black cities will be ploughed under. The engineer and the
manufacturer will live not to capture markets, but simply to provide
what men need [...] How, then, standing on The Beacon beside the
child of the future and knowing in my bones that the black cloud of
industrialism is passing from this land, how can I help seeing in this
view a vision of England redeemed, whatever storm and stress may
intervene, redeemed from the past five generations?

In this view, Bell was right about one thing: to toil in commercial factories was indeed not to be an Englishman's – or Englishwoman's – destiny. However, far from the cities being 'ploughed under' in a rebalancing of the relationship between the urban and the rural, their power grew, and with it their influence on the countryside. As a consequence, although the traditional manufacturing that made these 'black cities' declined dramatically in Britain during the second half of the twentieth century, Bell's hope that we may instead create a society that prioritizes what we need, rather than what we want, has certainly not been achieved.

Instead of an England 'redeemed' from the economic and social divisions wrought in the fires of the industrial revolution, the 'markets' are all powerful in an unrelenting growing culture of capitalist consumerism. Together with the concerns attendant with burgeoning industrial agriculture, it is this growing culture that Bell presents and examines in *A Suffolk Harvest* and in his autobiography, *My Own Master.*

※ 7 ※

A GROWING SEPARATION:
THE COUNTRY AND THE CITY

As had happened during the mid to late 1930s, interest in rural literature throughout the 1950s also waned. The resurgence of interest in countryside writing during World War II subsided, and the public's desire for an evocation of rural England – when the countryside was appreciated for both its sanctuary from, and its provision for, England's embattled cities – had cooled. Rationing came to an end in 1954, and there was a more pronounced sense that England's population was looking to the future and to modernity, not to the past.

As a direct consequence of the farm subsidies provided by the 1947 Agriculture Act, farming had moved even further from the traditional methods advocated by Bell and like-minded contemporaries such as Massingham. Instead, farms were becoming larger, more intensive, and more reliant on capital inputs in the form of machinery, artificial fertilizers and pesticides. Perhaps not surprisingly, his next book, *The Path by the Window* – a collection of articles from his column in *The Eastern Daily Press*, *A Countryman's Notebook* – was largely neglected by the wider reading public and received only local reviews.

In light of the technological, economic and cultural changes of the late 1950s and early 1960s, Bell's publishers wanted him to move away from writing about what they regarded as overly nostalgic, and address what they saw as more contemporary – more modern – concerns. Although his writing remained popular amongst his loyal readers

Workers at Rest

– his autobiography *My Own Master,* published in 1961, sold well (6,000 copies in the first year) – his other work, such as *A Suffolk Harvest* and *A Street in Suffolk*, sold poorly. And although his articles for the *The Eastern Daily Press* remained popular for his core readership, the decline in a wider interest in Bell's work beyond this readership reached a low point in the late 1960s when a collection of reflections called *As I See It* was rejected by his publisher, Faber, who called it 'altogether minor and mild'. Ann Gander notes that his writing at this point …

> … no longer appealed to city-dwelling readers so much […] Nowadays they were buying plastic goods instead of the old wood and metal, they wanted holidays by the sea, they wanted to watch television, listen to records, write with a biro pen. They wanted to see their lives moving quicker, not harp on about the days when the pace of life was slow and people were too. This generation had seen the world almost destroyed, and now they wanted to live for today.

However, despite the waning critical and public reception that his work received during this period, the quality of Bell's writing remained undimmed in the two publications I wish to explore in this chapter: *A Suffolk Harvest* and *My Own Master*. Rather than simply dismissing them as 'minor and mild', I would argue that they are in fact important contributions to the exploration of how the countryside, its communities and their relationship with the city, continued to change more profoundly than ever before.

A Suffolk Harvest was first published in 1956 and is, for the most part, a collection of articles – or versions of them – that first appeared in Bell's weekly *Eastern Daily Press* column. It is a book that sees Bell – now in his mid-fifties – reflecting on the passing of time and his own place in this society. He is no longer a working farmer, so these reflections – imbued with an increasing sense of mortality – bring with them a broader and deeper appreciation of day-to-day experience:

> It is hard enough in January not to wish myself in April. But when a man

is past fifty, can he afford to skip even a January and February? That is a thought to make him look around and make the best of today. If a snow-bearing wind bite his cheek, he can say, 'Here I am: I can feel it.'

It is this appreciation that underlies Bell's observations in this book, and develops the philosophical tone that is more apparent in his later works.

To provide a narrative drive across these diverse articles, the book is divided into twelve chapters, structured around a calendar year. Although the observations do not concern themselves to the same extent with the wider issues that he explored more explicitly in his previous two books, *The Budding Morrow* and *The Flower and the Wheel*, the insight that *A Suffolk Harvest* provides into English rural society is nevertheless significant. Thus, as well as considering the impact of increased industrial agriculture and, with it, the continuing marginalization of traditional husbandry, Bell also exemplifies in this work the ongoing lack of connection between the country and the city, and the erosion of rural culture.

In the opening chapter – entitled 'January' – Bell begins by quoting a line from Lord Raglan's book on the genesis of myth (*The Hero*), in which Raglan writes 'the very idea of a New Year is highly artificial. In nature the year has no beginning'. Immediately, Bell's aim is to highlight the false separation between humankind's constructed reality and his environment. Man may wish to impose a sense of order on the natural world, but it often has no significance beyond his perception: he cannot truly control his environment. It is significant that Bell makes this point on the opening page of *A Suffolk Harvest* – he wants to ensure that the reader is under no illusion concerning the negative impact that modern farming practices, which increasingly subjugate and manipulate nature through the use of machinery and the growing use of artificial fertilizers and pesticides, are having on the countryside.

He also wants to present how the communities that were once based around numerous, smaller farms have altered. In doing so, he stresses how quickly technological development has impacted upon almost every aspect of agricultural and domestic life:

Thirty-five years ago only one villager had knowledge of a power machine: the man who looked after the portable steam-engine for threshing. Since then the village families have bred tractor-drivers, tractor repairers, transport-drivers and clerks. They live in rows of new houses, with sewerage and television, and bird-baths and front lawns. [...] The only person who lives like a peasant is the retired don.

Here, Bell appears to make no explicit judgment about people's quality of life, and whether it has improved now that farming has become less labour intensive and has freed them up to become 'transport-drivers and clerks'. Nevertheless, the last line is illustrative of his wider view: modern conveniences are no substitute for a close connection with the natural world.

For Bell, like Massingham and Cobbett before him, the peasant is synonymous with a small farmer, and therefore the embodiment of effective husbandry. The peasant has a rich knowledge of rural experience and craft, and values tradition and works in harmony with the environment in which he lives. Thus, by likening a peasant to a retired don a figure emblematic of learned experience and culture – Bell is viewing and presenting them as social equals. The peasant is educated to the same extent as the academic, it is just that their education takes a different form. The implication here, therefore, is that because the retired don chooses to live like a peasant, a close connection with the natural world should be valued more highly than modern conveniences and luxuries.

Consequently, not only is Bell concerned about the practical implications of progressive farming that is driving people away from the land, he is also concerned about the ethical and cultural implications of a new breed of people who have 'bird-baths and front lawns'. They are moving away from a practical, sympathetic engagement with their environment towards an aesthetic one they can control, in order to meet primarily selfish needs. This shift firmly places man above the natural world, in that these people do not see themselves as equal to it, or even part of it. In this view, Nature is 'out there' and is to be used for our needs and pleasures; this is an ethical and cultural shift that has dominated the way we have viewed our environment ever since.

However, despite these burgeoning technological advances and the increasing movement away from rural communities to urban areas during the 1950s, the countryside – real and remembered – nevertheless remained deep in the psyche of many people. Although more and more people now lived in cities, many of these may have grown up in the countryside, or had parents and grandparents who lived their lives in rural communities. As a result, there was a shared memory, often passed down from generation to generation, of a different way of life that was rooted in rural communities and therefore in agriculture.

This emotional, even spiritual, connection to the countryside by those who live elsewhere is observed and presented by Bell in *A Suffolk Harvest* in a piece entitled 'Devoted Men'. He describes men who, having travelled overnight from their lives in Sheffield, arrive early in the morning of a Suffolk countryside with their 'vacuum flasks and tins' to settle for a day's fishing under the willow trees. He writes:

> Sheffield is a smouldering sort of city; it fumes away there in its bowl amongst the hills. These men must work in its pall, in foundries and factories. But what are they thinking, as they tend their great furnaces? They are seeing fat, silvery roach in quiet waters: they hear reeds rustle; they see green weeds waving, see the currents of the wind on the water.

Bell observes these men with a sense of sadness. He laments that they have to lead a life so far removed from one which appears to make them most contented – a sense of tranquillity that is found with a quiet interaction with the natural world. When these men have free time away from their jobs, they seek an escape from the smouldering city to the quiet waters of the countryside.

By presenting these 'devoted men' in this way, Bell is questioning the direction of a society that is encouraging this lack of connection. However, it seems to him that in the increasingly consumer-driven society in which he lives, fewer people appear to share his view. As capitalist consumerism strengthened its grip as the dominant ideology in post-war Britain, so labour was utilized to serve big business – the 'great furnaces' – rather than smaller communities that were more integrated with their natural surroundings.

Bell was a socialist, but he was also a realist. He understood that wealth must be created for the benefit of the national economy and society at large, and that consumers must be provided for. However, he could also see that because the majority of this wealth was created as a result of the urban consumer, those who lived away from these engines of capitalism were often viewed as less important, or simply misunderstood. Consequently, a growing urban population became more disconnected from the realities of the countryside – therefore the people who were primary consumers had a diminishing understanding of the challenges faced by rural communities.

When considering this growing lack of connection between urban and rural England in the 1950s, Bell uses the production of a basic necessity, milk, to illustrate this divide: 'To the Londoner there is grass and there is milk, and in between there is a cow. It's a perfectly simple, natural process: the cow does all the work, the farmer sits down under the cow twice a day and draws the profit.'

This lack of understanding compounded the economic challenges faced by farmers, in particular smaller farmers who could not avail themselves of the government support to the same degree as the ones who embraced more industrial methods of farming. Bell notes that the consumer is happy to pay a decent price for a man-made commodity, but baulks at paying for a food necessity: 'For some reason the man in Oxford Street will acquiesce in a huge pyramid of sales costs erected over, say, a hat or a pair of gloves, yet feels in some dim romantic corner of himself that milk should be delivered at the price at which it comes out of the cow.'

Such a disregard of rural communities – particularly of smaller farmers – has always been an issue in England, but it was becoming a more pronounced one as the second half of the twentieth century progressed. As food started to be regarded like any other consumable item, so farmers were forced to intensify and run their farms more like factories and businesses. The shocking scale of the damage to the environment these farming practices have caused has already been outlined. But in 'Devoted Men', it is the negative impact on both the individual and society that Bell is witnessing and attempting to convey. He is not simply depicting the desire for an escape from the 'smouldering city' to the 'quiet waters' of some long-remembered rural idyll. These men symbolize the disquiet and tension that an increasingly fragmented society was creating: the erosion of tightly knit, supportive communities and our relationship with the natural world.

Nevertheless, as the agricultural year draws to a close in *The Suffolk Harvest*, Bell conjures an image of the English countryside that is contrary to the way he sees it developing. In doing so, he exemplifies the value of diversity in the countryside, which was subject to increasing pressure as farming became more industrialized. He writes:

> England will still be England, I thought, while men continue to make heaps of mangolds, and while there are odd corners, neither paddock nor plantation, where a heap of mangolds and a stack can stand [...] I love these irregular, point-something-of-an-acre pieces left over from the jig-saw of commercial fields.

This somewhat nostalgic image of the 'heaps of mangolds' (one he also depicts in his first book, *Corduroy*) is particularly significant for him to evoke – it is a symbol of a dying husbandry.

He saw that progressive farming methods, together with the unrealistic demands of an increasingly disconnected and uninformed urban population, was leading to increasing specialization in agricultural practices on larger and larger farms. The small, mixed farms that he and others proposed almost twenty years earlier in Massingham's *The Natural Order* were becoming unsustainable in an era of subsidies aimed at larger, more intensive farms. The negative impact of this – soil degradation and the massive decline of wildlife – was yet to be fully felt, but Bell feared that the very character of England would be diminished if the diversity that was to be found in these 'odd corners' of its countryside was swept away in the name of progress.

Therefore if, as proposed earlier, English identity (or Englishness) is inextricably linked to the English countryside and the traditional practices of rural life – a rural culture – then such progress must also be challenging this identity. This idea that the creation of culture is more fundamental than what is conceived in the great towns and cities of England is exemplified by another rural writer contemporary to Bell, Lord Northbourne. In his own contribution to Massingham's *The Natural Order* Northbourne writes:

> All this chatter about the democracies have a degenerate culture! This will not be the case if the inhabitants of this island will grow their own bread, bake it and eat it, instead of reading their culture and letting others live to feed them. Is not culture the way you bake your bread? Does it not belong there?

He shares Bell's view that culture has been appropriated by those who live in the city, but that real culture is to be found elsewhere: in our fundamental interactions with the land and with each other.

This view is presented in the final chapter of *A Suffolk Harvest*, in which Bell describes a walk he takes 'in the fading light of one of the last days of December' through the fields of Grunsham parish, an area he knows well. He stops at a stile between two fields and reflects upon the year that has passed: 'Yesterday a sheaf of newspapers slipped out of a cupboard at my feet. Headlines of the past year swarmed before my eyes as I gathered them up. Crises between nations, threats of destruction, hopes of reaching the moon.' However, this wider context dissolves and seems distant – if not unimportant – as he contemplates a landscape that is so familiar to him.

At this moment he feels a sense of continuity – consistency – that only a close connection with a familiar natural environment provides. As in the course of his walk he pauses again for refreshment at a pub called 'Mulberry', he sees this connection to the earth in those who work these fields: 'Men who quaff their beer on a bench with Grunsham clay on their boots talk a different language.' This 'different language' speaks of a shared purpose, in which men work sympathetically with each other, and work sympathetically with nature.

It is through these close relationships that genuine contentment can found. It is an interconnectedness of people and of place – a sense of community – that Bell sees and feels as a part of himself:

> Grunshams's fields are ploughed. Smoke is rising from the chimney of that house known as 'home'. The flat field is ploughed. Over its hedge the rising sun will flash like a diamond every clear winter's morning, as I have seen it do this score of years, and glitter along its furrows, and strike into a small, east-facing room that I have called my own.

English identity has culture at its heart. For Bell, this culture was not to be found in the city, it is found in the people and the practices of the countryside – it is in the ploughed fields, and by the hearth of a farm worker's fire.

Therefore two common threads that run throughout Bell's observations in *A Suffolk Harvest* are woven together at the very end of the book: the importance of local community, and the importance of place. These are inextricably linked for Bell, and both assume particular significance for him. He is witnessing a society in which not only divisions within small communities were widening, but so were the divisions between the country and city. The American writer Wendell Berry shares his concern for this increasing opposition, writing that:

> It is by the measure of culture, rather than economics or technology, that we can begin to reckon the nature and the cost of the country-to-city migration that has left our farmland in the hands of only five per cent of the people. From a cultural point of view, the movement from the farm to the city involves a radical simplification of the mind and of character.

In *A Suffolk Harvest* Bell is reminding us how important a sense of place is, and with it a sense of belonging, not only to our minds and our characters, but also to the culture and identity of England as a whole.

❀ ❀

Bell's next book, *My Own Master*, was first published in 1962 and is his autobiography. Consequently, it provides a fascinating exploration of how he views, as an older man, his various experiences as a farmer and those closely associated with farming. He was sixty-one at the time of writing *My Own Master* – forty years after he moved to Suffolk to start farming, and over thirty years since he starting writing *Corduroy*. In recollecting his early life as an apprentice with Mr Colville, and then as a farmer in his own right, the book provides the reader with an insight as to how the experience of living in a farming community has altered almost beyond recognition in his lifetime.

Although he covers some of the same ground that he covered in his earlier work, particularly in his rural trilogy, he is viewing it from a very different perspective. Time has passed, and with it, knowledge and experience has been gained. Thus Bell is able to identify trends that had their beginnings in his younger life. As a result, he develops themes explored elsewhere in his work. Specifically, he presents the increasing disconnection between people and the land due to the rapid decline of small farms, and the rise of 'food factories' that were beginning to dominate the landscape of post-war English agriculture, and were symbolic of this disconnection.

In his Foreword, Bell makes a marked distinction between the countryside he found when he started farming as a young man in the 1920s, to the one he sees now: 'Rural England was still around us, before agricultural buildings were assessed for rates as food factories.' The life of 'Rural England' as Bell first found it – whatever the negative aspects of its reality – has changed forever with the creeping influence of outside business interests and a movement of its people towards towns and cities. As rural communities were fragmenting, so was, for Bell, the sense of a cohesive identity of 'rural England'. The sense of community that he so valued when he began his life as a farmer's apprentice in Suffolk is one of the defining characteristics that engender the identity not only of rural England, but of England as a whole.

When looking back in *My Own Master* to his first year as a farmer's apprentice with Mr Colville, he was contented to find that the lack of 'community spirit' that had troubled Bell in his life before moving to Suffolk appeared to be in abundance, whilst the pretension that can plague urban social mores was seemingly largely absent. He writes:

> I learned many things on that farm which I had not learned at school or at home. That there was a language more vital than correct speech. That there was a wider geniality than the nervy relationships of my own parental family. Here, people rode up on horses and dropped in to breakfast. My parents were out of touch with the people who inhabited the houses around them. [...] But in the country, barring a few misfits, everybody knew everybody and visited frequently, within the boundaries of their class.

This 'wider geniality' that Bell found was in contrast to his experience at home, and particularly at Uppingham, the public school he attended and disliked. He immediately appreciated the sense of community and informality, the absence of which had clearly previously stifled him. As an apprentice, Bell found himself part of the yeoman class – the 'most gregarious of rural classes', whose morality – in his words – was Edwardian, and whose religion was Low Church. Primarily, it was a class whose life was defined with a physical relationship with the land on which they lived and worked – 'life was flesh and grass'. In addition to the sense of community, and a greater ease between people that he desired and found, the fundamental relationship that this 'yeoman class' had with the countryside was a revelation to Bell. It was a way of life with a clear sense of purpose, and one that he knew he could come to value.

Thus, Bell recounts that despite the inevitable struggles most farmers had throughout the early twentieth century to make a living, when he arrived at Mr Colville's in 1920, 'everything which had belonged tradi-tionally to country life still continued'. Although as he latterly admitted, he may have had a somewhat 'sentimental view of country life' before he arrived, he was also realistic about the hard life this was for most that chose it: 'The rewards of farming were uncertain and hard to come by, except in war-time; a substantial farmer might have very little loose cash he could actually lay hands on; it was all locked up in soil and tackle.'

By the autumn of 1921 this uncertainty had reached new levels; farming hit a crisis point with the repeal of the Corn Production Act. This led to a fall in prices, and in turn 'that whole structure and technique of society withered away.' He could see the economic and social impact of this all around him in Suffolk:

> In the old town of Sudbury, beautiful big houses with forest trees in their gardens could be bought for five hundred pounds. Heavy-land farms were going out of cultivation. A farm in Benfield was abandoned altogether. Tramps dossed in the house, the fields grew waist deep in weeds. [...] What a time. Land for nothing but payment of a tithe. Riots against tithe itself.

As Bell reflects on the depressing effect of this repeal forty years on, he writes 'I am astonished at the speed of it. A century of established prac-tice was destroyed in ten years. Those who stuck most resolutely to their high old farming were the first to be ruined.' Consequently, he could see that those who sought to run small-scale traditional mixed arable and livestock farms would struggle to survive without outside support. With the hindsight Bell now had, he could see that a new breed of farmers was needed if they were to survive financially in the late 1920s and early 1930s, a breed that embraced specialization and 'progressive' methods of agriculture.

He cites the example of two brothers who survived the economic depres-sion at this time by farming 'six hundred acres on the Cambridgeshire chalk by tractor cultivations, growing corn after corn with artificial manures and [having] no livestock but a cat'. Small-scale, diverse and labour-intensive farming was giving way to larger-scale mechanization, specialization and intensification. Those who did not – or in most cases could not – follow this path had no choice but to give up their way of life. Bell notes that 'By 1929 I met a man who had farmed a thousand acres running a cottage tea garden. Another was selling lubricating oil.'

It was at this time of a severely struggling rural economy – of declining prices, and money owed from farmers to suppliers and craftsman – that Bell acquired his own farm, the experience of this recounted initially in *Silver Ley* and *The Cherry Tree*. Like the Cambridgeshire brothers, he knew that in such an economic climate he would need to adapt if he were to survive as a farmer. However, he also knew that this would be challenging for him because he did not believe that farming should be heading down a path to industrialism. Farming, he writes, is first and foremost about husbandry:

> I was the youngest disciple of the old order of farming. I had been taught by those shrew Colvilles that that was the way to farm, which had hardly changed from the way of the high-farming mid-Victorian farmers, and I applied the lesson. How was I, having learnt all this, and Fream's *Elements of Agriculture* (1911) almost by heart, to throw over the whole technique, and rethink my farming from the bottom up in a matter of a few years? [...] Never was a less revolutionary-minded person than myself, and hardly a less mechanical.

As much as he wished to follow the 'old order of farming', it was becoming increasingly clear that running diverse smaller farms was no longer economically sustainable. He quickly understood that if he was to make a success of his farm he must embrace, to a certain extent, new farming practices and new technologies.

One of the most significant of these developments was the arrival of the tractor. Bell notes, however, that at the time many farmers greeted its arrival with deep-rooted scepticism. Like generations of farmers before them, the primary power they had used to work the land was with horses, and they could not see the benefit of replacing – or supplementing – this traditional pillar of husbandry. His own farming community, like many other farming communities, was resistant to its introduction: 'Stubbornly my parish resisted the coming of the tractor. "That play heck with this heavy land," the parish said.' Based upon the farming theory and practice that Bell had so far gained, he shared these reservations to a certain extent:

> And by all the known laws of husbandry, two tons of iron plunging about on the tilth built up through years should have ruined it. The reaper-binder has been the only innovation for a hundred years which has 'worked'. How were they to know that these clumsy iron horses would 'work'?

Like his fellow parishioners, Bell was primarily concerned with the effect that such heavy machinery would have on the precious soil – they feared that it would become compacted and, over time, less able to promote and sustain crop growth. Their fears have proved to be well founded.

Therefore Bell identifies in *My Own Master* that there was a clear sense that the coming of the tractor to the field could be a watershed moment in agriculture if it 'worked'. The question beyond the concern of their impact on the soil was simply whether these 'iron horses' would be able to do the job as well as the real ones that had dominated the agricultural landscape for centuries. Of course, Bell's observation is recounted with the knowledge that tractors did indeed 'work', and their subsequent popularity revolutionized farming throughout the mid-twentieth century. He notes the extent of their impact when he looks back at the time he first worked for Mr Colville: 'When I went to him in 1920 there was only one power machine in the whole parish, and that was a portable (that is, horse-drawn) steam-engine for threshing; and he was the most advanced farmer in the parish. That is the measure of the farming revolution.'

As Bell moves to the early 1940s in his autobiography, he describes his second experience of day-to-day farming. He recollects that the farm he took on, Road Farm, was at the time a mixture of 'ancient and modern' methods, and that ploughing with horses often worked side by side with tractors. However, he notes that just twenty years later, these 'ancient' methods had all but disappeared from English farms. Therefore in less than forty years, 'power machines' had changed the practices of farming more profoundly than ever before.

The rise of the tractor certainly challenged the 'known laws of husbandry' that farmers had followed for centuries. For the first time in history a farmer had the power to wrestle and submit the land to his will, rather than develop a deep appreciation of it that traditional methods of husbandry foster. Bell illustrates this appreciation with reference to Road Farm: 'Round and round that field we walked all day. I came to know that hay intimately, every ingredient of it: clover, rye-grass, cocksfoot, and the occasional pallid corpse of a plant of chicory. I was soon in a state belonging to my former unmechanized farming.'

Here, Bell is again emphasizing the importance of developing a close relationship with the land that is worked. This harmony between the land and the farmer that 'unmechanized farming' facilitates is inevitably compromised with the arrival of large machinery. And so, together with other developments in agricultural methods, the tractor and its associated implements significantly altered the relationship that the majority of farmers had with the land they worked. Bell foresaw the environmental consequences of this changed relationship in his earlier writing, and exemplifies it in his later work.

Although the 1920s and the 1930s proved to be a difficult economic climate for most farmers, Bell also recognizes in *My Own Master* that this led to the availability and inexpensive cost of land, providing opportunities for others to speculate and ultimately to capitalize. In a chapter entitled 'The Cherry Tree' – ironically due to its evocation of the title of the final book of his rural trilogy – Bell introduces us to a young man called Rayner, who arrives in Suffolk in the early 1920s after buying three hundred acres of 'bleak clay soil'. He was looking to buy another seven hundred acres, and wanted to grow fruit on all of it.

The local farmers, who did not grow fruit on anywhere near this scale, were sceptical, and suggested that he would be better off away from the biting east winter wind, suggesting he should set up in Somerset, Hereford or Worcestershire. Contrary to their view, Rayner believed a cold east wind would actually benefit the fruit, as the colder winters would hold the blossom back, and so the fruit would escape the later frosts. Bell then observes what, in many ways, is a case study for how the second agricultural revolution would take shape in rural communities such as his.

Firstly, he notes that outside investment has always been necessary to begin any significant agricultural project:

He was from big business, and was prepared to pour large capital sums into that land in the belief that it would eventually produce a turnover per acre undreamed of before. This was an historical process [...] whereby always in the history of this country it has been money from industry, even since Tudor times, which has capitalised new developments in agriculture.

Secondly, Rayner would embrace every modern and developing method of 'progressive' farming available to him in order to cut labour costs and improve the efficiency of production. To start with, he would not have a single horse on the farm – instead he would use tractors to pull the cultivators. He would not grow crops between the rows of fruit trees, instead he would keep the earth bare and fallow because he believed it was not economically worthwhile, particularly with the big machinery he was using. He also lined his orchards with barbed wire, gassed the rabbits in their holes, and cut down woods that were providing a home to countless species of wildlife because he believed they harboured fruit pests.

Rayner was very much the epitome of the new breed of farmers who, Bell could see, would best survive the move towards industrialized agriculture. For Bell, Rayner is a good example of the impact this move would have, and he describes the scene of Rayner's rapid destruction of the local husbandry and, with it, the destruction of the local ecology:

> He filled in the sacrosanct drainage ditches, rooted out the hedges,
> laid field to field, and farm to farm, as he progressed with the acqui-
> sition of the landscape, until a thousand acres was to all intents one
> great orchard, patrolled by fruit-spraying machines with propellers,
> like aircraft without wings, which made a noise like aircraft as they
> whirled the spray around [...] Rayner demolished what we called the
> beauty to make the paid man prosperous. There was a war on trees
> (other than apple trees), birds, insects – everything but fruit.

In the name of agricultural progress, Rayner had turned a diverse habitat
into a monoculture. It was to be one of many, and countless others were
created across the English countryside as farmers like him rejected traditional husbandry – supported by government policy – in favour of a new
order of farming. As agriculture was transformed into agribusiness, so
the land was seen as a commodity, rather than something that is part of
a wider ecology. It became something to exploit, rather than to look after.

When Bell looks back in *My Own Master* and evaluates the effect
that farmers – or rather businessmen – such as Rayner have had on the
land and its communities in general, he could see it was a profound one.
Traditional practices of husbandry were not only marginalized, but were
wholly rejected, in many cases remarkably swiftly, in favour of methods
viewed as more 'progressive'. Bell, however, could not see how such
'progress' has been beneficial:

> So this was what the destruction of the old order had been for, and was
> bringing forth, with its huge concrete apple-grading and packing plant,
> its mechanical piggeries, its new bungalows, it house-sized square piles
> of apple boxes in the field. [...] Benfield (St George) became a complete
> example of the revolution in English agriculture, from the yeoman
> riding round on his cob to the farm worker coming to work in his own
> car, all in a dozen years.

As a consequence of these rapid changes – the 'destruction of the old
order' – the impact of such a revolution in farming was not only an

environmental one: it had significant ramifications for the economic and social fabric of rural communities. Fruit pickers, for example, are seasonal, which provided little security for local workers; instead, this work was done by young men and women from further afield, often students. This was indicative of the fact that there was little future on the land for the children of those who had previously sought their living from it. Instead, 'the sons of the old rabbiters, thatchers and bell-ringers grew up to become clerks, mechanics, truck drivers'. In order to pursue these jobs, people often had to move away from where they had grown up, thus dissipating rural communities, communities that would further dwindle as older generations passed away.

By 1962 Bell was acutely aware of the growing separation of the country and the city, and feared for the long-term environmental and social consequences of this disconnection. This was not only true for those who no longer worked with the land directly – the clerks, mechanics, truck drivers – but also for those who did: the students and the farm workers who now arrived for work 'in their own cars'. Because farming was becoming more akin to a 'job' and the countryside becoming merely a place of work, its status as a vocation – indeed 'a whole way of life' Bell states, 'which has persisted for centuries' – was being challenged. This inevitably led to a diminished personal investment in the countryside, and a growing separation from it. This is not to say that people no longer valued the countryside, but it suggests, as Bell did, that they developed 'schizophrenia' towards it. Thus Bell observed that the individual's – and society's – view of the countryside became an increasingly polarized one: it was 'either a food factory or a nature reserve'.

Once again, Bell used the example of Rayner to illustrate this growing polarization. Because Bell regards Rayner as a perfectionist and a convert to the new order of farming, when he and others like him take to farming they go, as Bell puts it, 'super-scientific', leading to the industrial orchard described above: nothing must be allowed to get in the way of efficiency. However, Bell also acknowledges that 'he was no grasping peasant, but a lover of nature' who on a day off would visit the 'naturalists' paradise of Wicken Fen, and lie among the butterflies'.

Rayner's apparently contradictory behaviour, in which he decimates a natural habitat on the one hand whilst showing a deep appreciation of a different habitat on the other, is indicative of the increasingly schizophrenic attitude we have developed towards the countryside over the past eighty or ninety years. Indeed, this conception of it as 'either a food factory or a nature reserve' is arguably as true in 2018 as it was when Rayner was both destroying and enjoying the countryside in the early 1920s. Like Rayner, we want an aesthetically pleasing countryside that we can enjoy, or even 'escape' to when it suits us. Indeed, Bell comments that a strong desire to maintain a connection with the natural world will remain in increasingly urban and suburban populations: 'The more we live by machines, the more we want wild nature alive to live with.' However, there is very little desire amongst these populations to develop a thoughtful understanding of the environmental, economic and social issues that rural England faces.

In the penultimate chapter of *My Own Master*, entitled 'Moonlight Sonata', Bell reflects upon this uncertainty with reference to the farmers of Grunsham, whom he described earlier in *A Suffolk Harvest*. In contrast to the deep-rooted connection that they had with their land, and the sense of place and identity they got from this connection, in the following extract we see a practical, emotional and spiritual removal from it. He writes in response to reading an article in his local newspaper on the developments in modern farming, and juxtaposes very different images of agriculture:

> … it was the nature of Grunsham folk, ordinary folk, men of the plough, to feel God in ears of grain, and earthly parables. Now accord-ing to a leading article in my East Anglian paper, 'as far as output is concerned farming is becoming just one end of an industrial chain that leads on to the processing and packaging plant, and thence to the self-service store.' Some farm buildings are now rated as food factories. So I don't know how Grunsham people will feel about the produce of their fields in the future.

The religious, or spiritual, connection in which God is felt in 'ears of grain, and earthly parables' illustrates the potent relationship these farmers have with their immediate environment. However, the 'food factories' that are increasingly populating the fields of Grunsham are far removed from traditional methods of husbandry, and symbolic of a way of life that is no longer sustainable. As agriculture becomes another arm of big business, so the land on which the people of Grunsham lived and worked – and on land like this all over England – is no longer valued as a place to create and live life. Instead, these farms and their fields become a necessary capital resource at 'one end of an industrial chain'. As a result, the sense of identity, of place and of pride that this land created in the people who lived on it and worked with it, was being lost in the ongoing intensification of the countryside.

In the book's 'Epilogue', Bell further emphasizes this loss, and likens the countryside to a 'vast factory floor' when he writes:

> I stood in the windless calm of the autumn evening and heard the heartbeat of the countryside, the throb of many machines out of sight, which does not cease till dark. Shut one's eyes, and one might be standing on a vast factory floor [...] I could not but be aware of this altered rhythm, having known the former rhythm in my lifetime.

Writing from the perspective of 1962, Bell could clearly see that he had witnessed 'a social and a technological revolution in my lifetime'. It is this revolution that has altered the rhythm of the countryside, and it is this 'altered rhythm' that Bell is ultimately concerned with, for it represents a loss of identity, place and pride in rural communities. For centuries, the 'heartbeat of the countryside' has been a steady one, but the rapid changes in farming methods – 'the throb of many machines out of sight' – throughout the mid-twentieth century were changing it forever.

In one of the last passages from the book, Bell illustrates the significance of these changes, and their impact on the rural communities he knew so well, when he describes a visit to his old village Benfield St George. In this recollection, Bell sees Jim Colville – the youngest of Mr Colville's sons, now an old man in 1962 – enter a cottage that would have once been a 'poor old place' only fit for the poorest of farm labourers. In recounting seeing Jim, he notes that having retired from farming 'he had bought it (now designated "ripe for conversion") and restored it like the rest, and furnished it with old oak, and hung an antique lantern in the porch. This struck me as the quietest and the most surprising revolution of all.'

This creeping gentrification continues till this day: elements associated with countryside traditions are packaged and marketed for new generations nostalgically seeking to create a more 'authentic' place to live. For Bell, Jim Colville encapsulates the changes he has witnessed in his lifetime: not only revolution in farming methods, but also a radical transformation of the structure, purpose and culture of rural communities.

Like all autobiographies, *My Own Master* is about time passing and the changes this passing brings. Forty years on from his first farming experiences, he sees that the way of life that he so valued at that time is no longer possible: the second agricultural revolution had altered everything. By 1962, Bell could see that the way of life on the land he sought and found in 1920 was, for the most part, gone.

Despite his lament for the changes that time has wrought to his beloved countryside and its inhabitants, and his worries for the future if we continued down this path of industrial agriculture, as an older man he remains philosophical and grateful for the things that remain unchanged and constant: 'How short a time we have here to work in after all, as [Alfred] Munnings said to me in Stradbroke church; and "What is it all for?" How splendid it must be to be free of the fear of time's passing and our body's decay, and reversal of fortune. Yet as I look out of my window at another spring, and the prospect of another summer, I know I love life more than ever.'

❦ 8 ❦

THE ALTERED RHYTHM OF THE LAND

BELL CONTINUED TO WRITE each week for *The Eastern Daily Press* throughout the 1960s and early 1970s, and his last book, *The Green Bond*, was published in 1976 – less than four years before he died. It was largely comprised of articles that had recently appeared in his column for *The Eastern Daily Press* (*EDP*), which in addition to his books, was his main literary output throughout the second half of his writing life. This was in the form of weekly articles that appeared under the title of 'A Countryman's Notebook'. His son, Martin Bell, noted that these articles 'appeared every Saturday on the editorial page with hardly a break from 1950 until a month before his death in 1980. They were treasured items that reached a far wider audience that the *EDP* itself. Perhaps uniquely, he was a regional columnist with a national readership.'

From these weekly columns, three collections of his articles were published during his lifetime: *Music in the Morning, A Countryman's Notebook* (1975) and *The Green Bond* (1976). A further collection, again entitled *A Countryman's Notebook,* was published posthumously in 2001 to celebrate the centenary of his birth. Like his books, the subject matter of them can be varied – however, his focus never strays too far away from the communities and the countryside of his beloved Suffolk. Consequently, many of the themes that he presents and explores in his books are also touched upon in his articles. With this in mind, I have chosen to focus on a selection of his later articles, primarily from the late 1960s and 1970s, as they form the body of his published output after *My Own Master.*

Resting Figure

As the title suggests, *The Green Bond* is a book about Bell's relationship with nature, and draws on over fifty years of experience of farming and living in the countryside. It is a celebration of what he calls 'a green bond' between people and the world around them. His belief that 'while we are alive, we live through things called insensate: petals, knots in wood. We are friends through our wildwood friends: it is a green bond' arguably grew stronger as he got older, and it was a belief he certainly expressed more explicitly in his later writing.

However, as Bell increasingly portrayed in his writing, it is a bond that he believed had weakened throughout the second half of the twentieth century. During World War II, numerous soldiers took to war with them a copy of Bell's first book, *Corduroy*, which evoked not only a vivid picture of the countryside, but also a way of life that they were fighting for and one day hoped to have for themselves. However, in less than forty years, Bell had witnessed an English countryside irrevocably changed by a society encouraged – through rising consumerism and technological progress – to value other things more.

In *The Green Bond*, Bell realizes that his earlier portrait of rural England depicted in *Corduroy* has faded into memory:

> Only the Black Death in the past has so decimated a countryside as modern farming as done [...] As fields are amalgamated for the huge machines of agri-business, creating savannahs, I think of the letters from serving soldiers whose dearest wish was to subsist on a few acres of English soil after the war and live in thankfulness simply for being alive.

The relationship between business and farming had strengthened immeasurably during the post-war years, and became inextricably linked. The increasing demands that capitalism was having on the countryside meant that farmers had little choice but to adopt modern farming methods in order to make a living. In order to do so, they had to invest significantly in modern technologies that were deemed necessary to farm the land – pesticides, fertilizers, tractors and machinery. However, the 'savannahs'

– the monocultures – that these business models and economies of scale were creating in the English countryside were far removed from the green and pleasant land that serving soldiers, some of them sustained by Bell's depictions in *Corduroy*, longed to return to. Moreover, as 'Englishness' is constructed with visions and values closely associated with rural, not urban England, this decimation of the countryside went beyond environmental concerns: it was also a challenge to English identity.

Therefore, if a citizen's identity is significantly constructed through his or her relationship with (or vision of) the countryside, the profound changes that Bell was witnessing would inevitably lead to a questioning, and perhaps altering, of this identity. As agriculture became agribusiness, so the land itself – the countryside held so dear in the hearts of generations of English men and women – was being viewed in different terms by an increasingly urban population. In this view it was becoming a commodity, and just another element in the process of inputs and outputs.

Bell highlighted this view with reference to the production of one of society's basic needs: milk: 'Once again, dairy farmers are faced with the question, how can one man be got to milk more cows than ever before?' As land was increasingly viewed merely as a means of production, the bottom line was efficiency – as much as possible for the least cost. With the increasing application of such business models, there was very little regard for those who had worked closely with the land for generations, or for the traditional husbandry they had practised, which had protected the welfare and ecology of animals and the environment.

In addition to the significant negative impacts on specific environments, such a mantra of production and efficiency did not benefit those who still had the opportunity to work the land. Bell notes in *The Green Bond* that despite all the business rhetoric and the farmers' investments, making money – at least for the farmer – remained challenging. He notes that 'For most of my adult life, farming has been in a slump. [...] Only during the war and just after it, has farming been prosperous.' Rather, they simply took on – under the guise of progressive farming – more of the labour individually, which, over time, drove people from the land and broke apart rural communities that had existed for centuries.

This was compounded by the wider structural arrangements – initially the 1947 Agricultural Act, then latterly the Common Agricultural Policy – that were increasingly encouraging industrial farming practices and hastening the fragmentation of rural communities. As traditions, crafts and mutually dependent economic and social relationships diminished in this new order of farming, so the culture of the countryside significantly altered. Therefore in *The Green Bond* Bell revisits the main reasons for this change in rural culture, focusing initially on the fact that the labouring population moved away from the land due to mechanization:

> Since labour has been mechanized, the sympathetic nerve has gone out
> of the sight of other men's work. A cube of straw flung out of a baler is
> a neuter shape, unlike the wheatsheaf which a man has to stoop to pick
> up, and then stoop to pick up another, and clash the two together to
> stand sturdily [...] To me, every field full of shocks of corn I saw was a
> static expression of labour, sweat, backache, thirst.

This 'sympathetic nerve' that is missing from farming is, for Bell, at the heart of rural culture. It suggests a purpose and care in work. It elevates seemingly simple day-to-day tasks to a craft, entailing a pride in the work.

However, to immediately undercut the above vision of an industrialized agriculture, *The Green Bond* opens with a description of Bell catching sight of himself in 'the great blank window of an Employment Office' whilst out shopping. He decides that he must pay a visit to his barber to rid himself of his 'rebellious locks', and must seek to replace his 'gipsy trousers'. The reaction of his friend Sighile upon seeing the new-look Bell, sets the tone for many of the subsequent observations in the book: 'You and I are peasants,' she said (Bell evoking the peasant of *A Suffolk Harvest*). 'We are the past, but we are also England's future, after the Hour of Truth, which is soon, and the death of money. Then for the day of nettle juice, grass juice, wild thyme, impregnating gipsy skirts and peasant trousers, and "many a green gown", hand sown every button, every stitch.'

Although the 'Hour of Truth' is not made explicit by Bell, what he is questioning in these opening pages is the value of progress that is driven by capitalist consumerism. For Sighile, Bell's makeover is symbolic of the rise in consumerism that is damaging people and the environment in which they live, and his gipsy trousers and rebellious locks are the antithesis to this emergent culture. It is also recognition that a society that prioritizes money, and is created with this at its heart, is not a sustainable one: it is a flawed ideology. Rather, through this interaction with Sighile, Bell presents a need to return to a more traditional – natural – state of being in which we develop a greater appreciation of the world around us. In this appreciation, we should strive not to consume our resources, but rather to work with them – valuing traditional crafts above mass production is an important example of this.

This is why he evokes the idea of peasantry, for despite its negative connotations, this state of being is a sustainable one, and is largely at odds with an increasingly consumer-led society that is encouraged to embrace technological progress. Through this evocation, he is suggesting that we need to understand that a pursuit of money, which appears to dominate England's present in *The Green Bond*, is superficial – it is not Truth, and will not lead to a future England that best serves either its citizens or its environment.

For Bell, this pursuit of money is not just about the rise of consumerism in towns and cities: it is also about the effect of the continuing capitalization of the countryside. For example, Bell describes cycling along a Suffolk lane on a May morning, when he emphasizes the impact that a move away from more traditional methods is having on the countryside he knows so well:

Clouds of spray exude from machines, killing weeds and anaesthetis-ing the breeze as it wafts this way. But bordering this by-way they can still be called wild flowers, unless some local authority condemns them also to be sacrificed to god-the-motor-car. The trees that have been felled to appease him don't bear thinking of.

The vocabulary Bell employs here – 'exude', 'killing' 'anaesthetising', 'felled' – leaves the reader in no doubt that to his mind the natural environment is being 'sacrificed' in the pursuit of progress.

Indeed, this artificiality and its negative impact on the environment is brought into sharper relief by Bell when he is further into his journey across the countryside, when he sees, to his satisfaction, 'a rolling sea of green corn', which indicates to him a more sympathetic husbandry: 'I pass a field of oats whose broad blades and blue-green vigour speak of pigs. I know of old that hue of health. It is organic.' Rather than dominating the countryside through 'clouds of spray' exuding from machines, this 'hue of health' is indicative of agricultural practices much more akin to Bell's early farming life in which he sought to work in harmony with the land.

Bell is not being nostalgic about 'England's past': rather, he fears for England's future. By the time he was writing *The Green Bond* in the mid-1970s, the wider impact that the post-war intensification and mechanization of agriculture was having on the English countryside was becoming clear. The scrubbing of hedgerows, mechanization, artificial fertilizers and the use of pesticides were creating monocultures that drastically reduced the variety of species that were able to survive. Indeed, he was bearing witness to the quickest and most significant destruction of ecology in human history: a destruction that has affected all of us. Bell notes the impact of just one of these new 'inputs' when he writes: 'In the former days our fertilizer was farmyard manure, and our only herbicide was the hoe. Now we have high farming: even larger doses of synthetic nitrogen produce high yields of corn, which feed us, while the run-off from the fertilizers can poison us.'

However, Bell did not have faith in the policy makers to solve such wide-ranging environmental issues that were being created by a society – an economy – that demanded more 'efficient' food production: '[the air] is polluted by the speeches of politicians with little to communicate but who sneer at one another.' Instead, he believes that 'the only positive good sense, the only recipe for revival, is talked about by farmers'. For him, if English farmers are to feed a growing population in a sustainable way and 'double the output of England's still fertile soil', then they must be unshackled from the interests of big business and allowed to return to traditional farming methods.

He questions the dominant thinking that has led to the rise of agribusinesses, questioning the view commonly held by advocates of agribusinesses that the 'growth of populations stresses a need for bigger, better farms'. In this questioning, he argues that smaller-scale, organic farms can adequately address the needs of the consumers of this growing population: 'Dear friends, arms and legs on small plots of this earth can produce vastly more than your soil-compressing giant tractors. Look at allotments, at country gardens – the record yield of wheat this year was grown on a three-acre plot.'

Integral to this production is the organic nature of it. He notes the vibrant 'gigantism' of his broccoli in his own vegetable plot to illustrate that utilizing land for maximum gain can be done organically without the need for machinery or artificial fertilizers: 'Every leaf seemed to hold a pint of rain. This is the result on ground which was first under a deep-litter hut for hens [...] a nitrogenous intoxication.'

The benefits that Bell sees in a more traditional approach to farming is further noted in his thinly veiled criticism of modern methods of fowl husbandry when describing a gift from his sister and her husband: 'They have brought us a basin of eggs from their freest of free-range hens. They have a broad paddock to roam. They were bought as culls from battery cages; they even had to re-learn how to walk. Now they are sprightly, happy all day long, and lay copiously.' These 'culls from battery cages' – regarded as useless and dispensable in modern agricultural practices – are transformed by the care and attention associated with methods of farming that in the second half of the twentieth century were increasingly viewed as outdated.

This transformation and what it represents is significant because it questions the perceived efficiency of modern farming techniques, which were largely promoted by the multitude of agricultural businesses that make money from encouraging these techniques. Consequently, although not explicitly stated by Bell, he is suggesting in these observations that policy makers should reconsider the pathway on which farming finds itself – not least because if we are to feed a growing population, then intensive, mechanized farming is not the most effective way of doing so. Rather, it is a farmer's perceptive understanding of, and close connection with, the subjects that he farms that will provide for him, for others and for the environment.

Like much of his later work, one of the recurring themes in *The Green Bond* is a sense of loss, often in relation to either a physical or a spiritual removal from the land. For example, Bell recollects surveying his friend Bert's farm and seeing the 'new furrows glistening in the winter sun' in what was regarded as 'the best field in Redisham' – a field that has since been lost in pursuit of technological progress. As Bell observes:

> There were no 'amenities', but there was the earth. There was no telly, but we talked of the soil […] we talked of 'mowlds'. Bert made the mowlds of clay, with long patience of digging and ridging, so his acre became like fine fen land, and he grew master crops of spuds, kale and onions and beans. Today those mowlds cry out for sun, for air: Bert is dead; they suffocate under concrete: a petrol pump stands in place of his store-shed: the petrol pump is king.

As Bell reflects upon this scene, he questions the priorities that are driving these developments by asking if we want thriving rural communities that can efficiently provide a growing urban population with food in a way that does not destroy the ecology of the countryside, or do we want to suffocate it all under 'clouds of spray' and 'concrete'? As Bell notes, 'There were no amenities, but there was the earth' – it is the loss of connection with the earth that he laments, for it represents the green bond that sustains us.

It is clear from such observations that in the last decade of his life, Bell's commitment to social equality and the protection of the countryside's environment and rural communities was as strong as ever.

As a member of various committees hoping to influence positive change in local affairs, he was frequently frustrated with what he regarded as purposeless bureaucracy. He writes:

> So I have now and again tried to do my bit; sit on committees, study the minutes, raise any point 'arising from', as the chairman invites. Determine to keep a cool, clear head. But soon one finds oneself in collision with some bureaucratic ruling administered from afar [...] Soon the circulation quickens, the voice loses its cool rational tone. Instead of the good committee-man, I find myself once more the puny rebel hopping mad against this bureaucratic scheme of things entire.

The central frustration that Bell is illustrating here is one that was touched upon in Chapter One when he began his apprenticeship and felt useless in his new environment. During his first few weeks on Mr Colville's farm, he came to a deeper appreciation that 'education' takes many different forms. With this appreciation, Bell challenged the widely held notion that the education provided by conventional – and prestigious – institutions of learning was superior to a more practical, skills-based education. Consequently, over forty years later he struggles to accept decisions or policies made by people who do not have the relevant experience or understanding to appreciate the impact of them.

Clearly his experience of farming, and the increasing (negative) influence that he sees business has had on agriculture, greatly shapes this view: 'Am I the only romantic left who takes nature for his guide, who thinks a past generation of countrymen was more truly educated than many who can write "BA" after their names today? For whom eight-tenths of the "gross national product" is a multi-million-pound nightmare of gadgetry?'

Therefore, Bell also revisits in *The Green Bond* what he sees as an increasing disconnection between education and experience. If there is no practical application alongside of, or subsequent to this education, then it lacks a relevant purpose, and the 'truly educated' are *not* those who have remained in institutions of education until the age of twenty-one before seamlessly becoming the new generation of bureaucrats, administrators and 'committee-men'. In this view, such education frequently leads to a theoretical vacuum, often focusing on bureaucratic processes, rather than usefully informing practical outcomes.

In relation to Bell's concerns both as a farmer and as an advocate for rural communities on various committees, this separation of education and experience often meant that people moved away from the land, or from traditional crafts associated with the land – 'a past generation of countrymen' – and was part of the ongoing drift of people from the country to the city. As a further consequence of this drift, rural and urban populations became increasingly divided demographics: understanding between them declined, increasingly leading to decisions being made without the insight of experience. He illustrates vividly the opposition between the theoretical and the practical:

> Drought in America means that Food is said to be the watchword again. I can still wield a spade, as I did in London clay in 1916, in Suffolk clay in 1940, and in Waveney Valley loam here in 1973, 4, 5 … on to the Bennenium. How simple and wholesome is this issue. Let the 'Critics', Sociologists, Economists (who have in recent sessions confessed themselves clueless) take up spades – a million, ten million, twenty million spades, and get a taste of what it takes for a Tanzanian to get a living, or the Nigerian.

For Bell, the spade and the ability – and desire – to 'wield it' is hugely significant. Years of working closely with the land had deeply reinforced his belief in the importance of maintaining a practical appreciation of it – for the benefit of the land itself, and those who depend on it for their sustenance. This 'simple and wholesome' philosophy was also so important to Bell because he felt that not only would a growing separation lead to the theorizing of 'Critics, Sociologists, Economists', it would also further the cultural and intellectual divide between the rural and the urban.

To counteract this, Bell believed that the everyday elements of rural life needed to find a new appreciation, however this might be achieved:

'Let sculptors ponder a potato,' he suggests, 'and artists note that patch of rust on a barn roof in the buff harvest plain.' Only with a renewed appreciation would the status and value of a working countryside be raised.

However, by the 1970s England's population had never before been so far removed from such an appreciation, or so removed from their rural roots. The capitalist economic ideology that was shaping post-war English agricultural policy and society in general, hugely influenced this purposeful retreat from the land. However, Bell could not see how, in the long term, this could be a sustainable ideology, and he believed that we needed to maintain a close relationship with the natural world for the benefit of future generations: 'One day we shall all have to live in so simple a manner that we may be conversant again with the wheeling of the planets.'

As well as not being sustainable and resonant in value, he could also not understand how living an urban lifestyle with an increasingly predominant consumer culture was desirable. After getting caught in Norwich's rush hour ('we became a vertebra of an immense caterpillar. Ahead of us, a lump of industrial machinery which looked like an octopus that had died of convulsion') he questioned how modern society had evolved so that people had to make this journey twice every day. In addressing this question, he observed that more people than ever before were merely subject to the demands of a neo-liberal capitalist ideology. He writes: 'I was once shown over a factory. Processions of identical tins jogged around on tracks. At a junction of two tracks a girl sat with a stick, and when they got jammed there she beat them with the stick, and they moved on.'

This factory, and particularly this girl – who it is doubtful got any degree of satisfaction from this job – is symbolic of what concerns Bell. She is not only employed on low wages to carry out a mind-numbing task, she most likely has no interest in either her employer, or the product, or the consumer – her personal investment in a process on which she may well spend the majority of her working life is next to nothing; the 'sympathetic nerve' is missing. He writes:

We are cogs – we are all day making cans or putting things into cans: cans to nourish us: corned beef; cans to kill us: tanks. And after the day's work we become a procession of cans, bumper to bumper. How few in our society are not on their way from the human factory (1,000-pupil comprehensive) to the consecrated bin via automated conveyer track?

This is a particularly bleak sketch of English working society in the 1970s, and although many of the factories may have been replaced by expanding numbers of administrators and service industries, it is one that has lost none of its vivid authenticity in 2018. Then, as now, the majority of people in society have very little agency over their own lives because they are subject to the demands of political and economic systems that prioritize growth and efficiency, largely for the benefit of the few. As a result they become cogs in these systems, and, like the girl with the stick, have very little genuine personal or emotional engagement in their jobs. Of course, this does not apply to all. However, as Bell argues throughout his later publications, such disengagement has become more prevalent since the majority of society has turned its back on the countryside for anything other than as a place of food production and of leisure.

For example, Bell's observation of a new order in people's relationship with the land is exemplified when he recounts delivering a speech at the recent opening of a rural museum of old farm tools in 1974, a speech he no doubt lamented having to make at all: 'Look at all these handles. Do you see how thin they are worn, how shiny they are? [...] Think of all those men and women who turned all these handles, for hours and days and years, that we might stand here, fed and clothed.' Bell wants the assembled crowd to appreciate that the roots of any economic growth are to be found in the most fundamental of all humankind's interactions with the natural world: farming.

However, very recently – in Bell's working lifetime – this interaction has changed more significantly than ever before. The close relationship between man and the land that is symbolized in the worn handles of these old, now redundant tools has rapidly disappeared due to the industrialization and commercialization of agriculture. The old order of farming – and to a large extent rural life – that had existed and supported the population at large for thousands of years was being consigned to history, and its remains put on show for posterity.

Therefore, as the separation of the country and city widened towards the end of the twentieth century, with more and more people viewing the countryside as a place of leisure or in aestheticized or economic terms, so a dichotomy in the way that society regarded England's green and pleasant land increasingly emerged. On the one hand, like the tools in the farm museum, areas of the countryside were 'lovingly preserved in this England' (for example, through the creation of National Parks), as were country houses (through The National Trust). On the other hand, Bell rather caustically notes that a supposedly 'more "educated" population was also more ruthlessly set on beauty's destruction, with or without the consent of the planner, than at any time since William I's harrowing of the North'.

In addition to the massive impact that mechanization and intensification in farming practice was having on the countryside, Bell also exemplifies the increasing urban influence that was permeating rural England: 'Bulldozers, earth-gougers, plough across Constable's Dedham Vale as elsewhere. Contractors duly earn knighthoods. Thereafter come litter, broken bottles, transistors. This blessed plot....'

This increasing commodification of rural England went hand in hand with a rising culture of consumerism – the result of which was this contrasting and often contradictory view of the countryside. It was a place to be exploited and despoiled to meet the demands of modern society, but it was also a place (or designated parts of it) to be cherished and preserved by the same society.

This new order happened so quickly that the negative environmental, economic and social consequences of it were not fully felt in Bell's lifetime. However, he feared what they might be – with justification, based on his experience of working closely with the land and its rural communities. He questioned, and, to a certain extent, despaired at humankind's conscious movement away from the natural world that sustained him. He could see that he was placing himself above nature in his misplaced arrogance, writing that 'The goal of nature is man, it is assumed. But I prefer my father's view, that nature may yet supersede man with a wiser being, whose basic amenities will not require so much of this earth's miraculous soil.'

But having a close relationship with the land was no longer a priority in this modern progressive society. Instead, the 'earth's miraculous soil' was there to be exploited in whatever way Man deemed necessary. Those who did seek to maintain such a harmonious relationship – particularly in relation to farming – were often viewed as 'Luddites', who deserved to be left behind because they were resistant to the adoption of 'progressive' methods and new technologies.

Indeed, such 'simple' country folk were often satirized by others, who viewed them as socially and intellectually inferior: 'Why do country people lean over gates and stare? It has been the townsman's symbol of a rustic vacancy of mind, as you can see when you leaf through old editions of *Punch*.' For Bell, this view is sadly indicative of the ideology shared by an increasing number of people who have grown up without any experience of working or living in the countryside. Rather than having 'a rustic vacancy of mind', those who look upon their fields have the opposite intention:

> The gate-propper may be debating information supplied by his eyes about his fields, involving vital judgments. He may not even be consciously looking, but listening [...] anyone who stands still even for a few minutes here is made aware of communication going on between living things, inert substances and primal laws.

The close connection the countryman has with the land is evident: it is a fundamental one that should not be devalued and relegated below the priorities of a society whose primary focus is on the machinations of the city. Indeed, developing an appreciation of 'communication going on between living things' should be something that we all seek to achieve,

195

rather than drift – consciously or unconsciously – towards an increasing separation with the natural world.

❊ ❊

I would like to conclude this chapter by focusing on two of the last pieces that Bell wrote for the *EDP*, a little less than a year before he passed away. I have chosen these because in them Bell reflects vividly on what he loved most – his family aside – in life: farming. In the first piece, Bell visits a farmhouse that has been painstakingly restored by a couple: the house had fallen into disrepair after the farmer could no longer make a living from his small plot. For Bell, this farmhouse symbolizes tradition and also the changes to farming in England throughout the twentieth century:

> As I sat gazing around me in the big handsome rooms I thought how this, too, is a rich storehouse of centuries of the arable routine. I could almost hear the remembered tramp of feet, and husky words from throats dusty from the stack-yard. I felt a kindred spirit with the redolence of that old house. Although my half-century of labour on the land must be as a day gone by to those huge rafters, I too could claim to be something of a storehouse of memories of days before there was a single power machine in our parish, and the windmill was busy grinding corn on its rise in the view. It never occurred to anyone in that parish that this would not go on the same.

The scope of change Bell has witnessed as he contemplates the house's history and purpose has been immense. The rise of the 'power machines' of modern farming has changed everything, putting an end to the 'centuries of the arable routine' remarkably quickly.

Whereas he makes no obvious judgements about the disappearance of the parishes' traditional farming practices in this passage, in the second piece he makes explicit some of the consequences of these changes. Thus, in contrast to the poetic tone of the reverie above, Bell adopts one of disappointment and frustration – almost of anger. This tone is set as a result of seeing farmers around him carrying out an increasingly common practice associated with modern farming methods – setting fields on fire. This practice of burning straw stubble is carried out because it is deemed uneconomic to gather the straw and use it for any other purpose.

However, 'When farming was a civilized art, straw was a valued by-product' as it had a value for farmers because it was needed as bedding for livestock. But in a new age of livestock 'husbandry' it is no longer required because slurry is seen as the most efficient way to deal with animal waste. Burning fields and creating slurry are features of supposedly progressive methods – but for Bell, both practices are absurd:

> Concomitant with this incendiarism is the abhorrent 'slurry', which, the public has at last been warned, is running away through unauthorized channels and polluting rivers, even as the farmers' vast overplus of nitrates are poisoning wells. We avoided all this with cattle and pigs bedded deep in clean straw in our yards.

There is a whole system of traditional husbandry that is being unpicked – or simply neglected – by modern farming methods. By not following traditional methods, the modern farmer is creating needless problems that are damaging to the environment and to livestock. Animals are forced to stand in their own waste, which, rather than be mixed with straw and turned into manure to fertilize the land, is washed away – along with artificial fertilizers – to pollute the environment.

It is this disregard for the welfare of the land that Bell cannot abide. He knows that we cannot simply treat the environment like a factory that will keep producing for us. The negative consequences of years of intensification, then mechanization in farming are becoming hard to ignore in the most precious of all resources – soil: 'The soil has been compacted by decades of the heavy-wheeled tractor, into a surface like tarmac. I put it to the modern farmer that all he required of the soil was to be a medium to hold the fertilizer within reach of the roots of the plant. He rather agreed with me.'

In modern farming methods, the health of the soil was largely ignored. It was, as noted above, simply a substance to hold things together as they grow. Studies that argued for a greater appreciation and care for the soil – studies such as Alfred Howard's *An Agricultural Testament*, published in 1940 – shared Bell's concerns that a different approach, more akin to traditional methods of farming, needs to be taken if this damage to the precious soil is to stop and be reversed.

Bell stressed that a start would be to reduce artificial fertilizers that have no long-term value to the soil (excess nitrogen is washed away to pollute water courses) and use farmyard manure, which would also add much needed humus to the soil. Bell asks: 'So where does it all end? Surely we should at least make a start in a return to the way soil was regarded by farmers of my generation, as an asset that should receive back the straw, which is now so lightly consigned to the flames, in the form of farmyard manure.' If relatively small and inexpensive changes such as this did not start to take place, Bell feared for the future of both farmland and farmers themselves:

> Else, agriculture must become an automatic pursuit of the bigger and better machine, which, for its high cost, can still only do one season-able job, and is written off in yet speedier obsolescence. Some stability of practice is required, some injection of the organic principle, to establish the beginnings of the equilibrium in what is no longer just farming, but a huge investment in obsolescence which must some day and suddenly burst like a bubble. [...] And once they call the job husbandry.

To Bell and many like him, farming is not like any other job or business: it is husbandry. In such a view, making money is not the primary goal. Instead, the job of husbandry is to work with the land for the benefit of its ecology as well as for the benefit of the farmer and his 'business'. However, as the twentieth century progressed, this traditional vision of farming was fading in the 'automatic pursuit of the bigger and better machine'. As farmers were being encouraged to mechanize their production, so their overheads grew inexorably. This in turn forced them to intensify on a larger scale in order to justify the huge investments in the new technologies.

In this new order of farming, labour costs were the new enemy. In order for farmers to keep pace with the competition, mechanization was crucial so that they could work greater areas of their land more quickly. In this business model, labour had to be cut, which resulted in a fragmentation of rural communities. Not only were farmers being forced to leave their land because of economies of scale, so were the many craftsman who relied on a more traditional husbandry.

As agriculture became agribusiness, so the drift away from the values associated with traditional husbandry became increasing apparent. Bell observes a further example of this in *Music in the Morning*, another collection of *EDP* articles, published in 1954:

> The other day I was watching chicks coming out of an incubator. It was one of those monster machines which hatch an astronomical number of eggs at a time. The man in charge of it performed his task with an expert speed in which wonder at this mass of infant life had no part. Malformed or weakly chicks were knocked on the head and thrown aside in a moment.

The primary concern of farming has always been about producing food to provide for men, women and children, with the secondary concern being the welfare of the land and the animals. In this, there has been a fundamental understanding that the two are closely linked, with the appreciation that to safeguard quality food production and food secu-rity, the land must be looked after. However, the man in charge of the 'monster machine' carrying out his grim task is, for Bell, representative of the rupturing of this link between man and nature. Instead, the scene he describes – which could have been taken from an urban factory floor – shows the extent of this detachment, and is opposite to the relation-ship he believes we should have with the natural world: 'I am neither scientific nor mathematical, but there is a word that mathematicians use, "continuum". For me the word has a private meaning, of a sustained, quiet, complex activity.'

For Bell, this continuum is synonymous with husbandry. But as machines took the place of those who for generations have husbanded the land, this continuum was in danger of being lost forever. He could see that in these new 'progressive' farming methods, the 'sustained, quiet, complex activity' of his forefathers was no longer valued. This would prove to be detrimental not only to the English countryside, but in the long term, to us all.

❧ CONCLUSION: THE NATURE OF MATERIALS ❧

THE RENOWNED AND INFLUENTIAL critic F. R. Leavis once described Bell's writing as 'naïve, but naïve in the right kind of way'. Bell was pleased by this comment because in many ways this was what he was striving for in his writing. Perhaps unlike more fashionable, critically valued writers, he did not want artful, 'literary' construction to compromise a sense of authenticity in his work: for Bell, this would simply lead to style over substance and indirectness. Thus, writing meant very little for him if not rooted in fundamental reality: that is our reliance on – and being part of – the natural world. As his practical farming experiences were drawing to a close during the writing of *The Flower and the Wheel*, he reflects upon the power of literature to communicate ideas and fire the imagination:

> While I have been cultivating the soil [...] silently within the covers of unopened books on my shelves, the minds of men are mining in the realm of ideas, working like yeast, although the authors have been centuries dead. The ideas have their own life hidden away in those covers like the life of a seed. It is perhaps the most notable work of civilization that those small black hieroglyphics can, through a ray of light, transmit such a complex activity to the brain and nerve cells of a living man.

However much he values how writing can inspire and teach us from the minds of others across the centuries, he sees this worth diminished if literary construction and appreciation is purely an intellectual exercise. Such writing and reading is only worthwhile if it can be felt and lived

Suffolk Sky (Oil)

in our interaction with the world around us. Therefore, he attests the fundamental importance of grounding writing in physical primary experience, stating:

> And yet, without the earth and its crops, what are they, these ideas? [...] The ideas arising out of life must be incorporate in the flesh of new life. The absolute values must be felt in that flower and that clod: they must be corpuscles of the warm bodily flow. Else, literature is so much paper.

He acknowledges that we can learn from the ideas of others, but emphasizes that this learning is more valuable if these ideas are born out of a practical interaction with the world.

In other words, Bell questions the value of theorists whose ideas are abstractions rather than representative of experience connected to 'the earth and its crops'. And it is these 'absolute values' – values that are inextricably created through our interaction with the natural world – that underpin all that he writes. His experience as a farmer affords him a better position than most to appreciate them, and he believes that without this appreciation and an attempt to communicate it, writing has little value for him. Here, he provides an insight to how he would not have become a writer if he had not first become a farmer:

> I am constantly being told 'You should let other people do the sheer spade-work, the machine-minding, the cow-keeping; while you give yourself to higher things.' Creative literary work and so forth. They will never understand that nothing good can come out of a man in that way unless it is squeezed; unless there is a pressure almost as physical as that of a hand crushing the juice of an orange. And that pressure is only generated by actual frictional contact with life.

It is this 'pressure' of experience that inspired him: he could not see the point in writing if it became an abstraction, or a purely intellectual exercise away from 'actual frictional contact with life':

And how much frictional encounter in my case with corn and plough-share, with cow-byre and corn-bin is required to yield a drop here, a drop there, of honest and needful expression? It really takes about ten years of hard living to produce a real book.

If he were to write with any sense of truth about farming, then it must be rooted in authentic experience; one only need consider the minute detail in his unpublished notebooks to see how closely he observed life around him, which provided the raw material for his work.

In this view, he also believed that too often there is a false distinction made between intellectual and manual pursuits, and he could not understand why people regarded writing as somehow being 'higher' than farming. For him, they are inseparable. As a consequence, he revisits in his writing his criticism of those who regarded non-manual activities (such as writing) as superior to manual activities. For Bell, there needed to be a greater balance between them, and if this balance is not attained, he believes that people are in danger of losing touch with what is fundamentally important, which is a close connection to nature and a sense of place and community. He argues that if this is to be achieved, 'we need a plainer harness for our imagination, a humbler preoccupation for our highest powers. We need to return from our mental skies and understand the nature of materials. We are in danger of forgetting the ingrained nature of life.'

This desire for a 'plainer harness for our imagination' is evident within his own writing: he does not embark on flights of fancy to entertain. Indeed, this philosophy also echoes Bell's earlier observation regarding education: we should be seeking an intellectual life that fosters a reconnection with our environment, not one that takes us further away from it. For us to appreciate the 'ingrained nature of life' we must develop a relationship with the 'material' of the land, and he is critical of modern developments in agriculture that diminish this relationship: 'It is one of the drawbacks of the present tractor-plough that one turns one's back upon the earth. In the very touch and taste of things there are great lessons to be learned, to be relearned.'

He is once again stressing the importance of primary experience in relation to the environment. Here, Bell sees it as a connection with the land, and an appreciation of our dependence on it for our very existence: 'If we as a nation should, through circumstances outwardly adverse, become occupied and preoccupied with bread, our vital raw material, it will be a good thing for us. It should re-settle the ballast of our thought: it should give us truth.'

However, this truth – a deep appreciation of the natural world – was becoming lost in a society that was moving away from the 'very touch and taste of things' and becoming part of a culture of consumerism. It is this truth that Bell values and endeavours to convey in his work, not least in one of the last pieces he wrote towards the end of his life for his 'Countryman's Notebook' for *The Eastern Daily Press*.

In this piece, he describes meeting an old farmer of eighty-nine in Bury St Edmunds. The farmer remembers, as a youth, seeing country labourers – including his father – assembled around a blacksmith's fire one day approaching Christmas, standing idle. When the master of a local farm saw them, he asked why: 'Because we haven't any work, master, nor anything to eat neither, and not a bit of firing in our housen,' they replied. Upon hearing this, the master instructed them to go to his door where they would be fed and given work to do, for 'Everybody in this parish must have a Christmas dinner,' he said. Perhaps more than any other meeting or experience he recounts in his many books and articles, the way this old man had 'told me this so simply', affected Bell:

> When I got back, I wrote it down just as he spoke it. Years later, writing a book on farm life, I included it. It filled just a page. It is the best page in the book, and it was not my writing at all, but that of a man speaking, a horsekeeper's son who left school when he was about 12 years old.
>
> It still moves me to read it, because the man spoke so naturally, without conscious art; it was his life.
>
> And it is literature. When today pundits speak of Culture, I just wonder what it is they think they are talking about.

This passage – together with the description Bell wished to reproduce verbatim from the farmer's recollection – illustrates the concerns at the heart of Bell's writing. Not only does he want to give a voice to rural figures often overlooked or idealized, he also seeks to foster a greater appreciation of what is being lost in a context of such rapid change in the countryside. Longstanding communities, and the values and traditions that underpin them, were fragmenting. A way of life that had existed largely unchanged for hundreds of years was disappearing, and with it a rural culture that could never be reclaimed. In an increasingly urban society, for many, culture is something to be found in the city, not in the country. Bell, however, who had lived all his life working and writing about the land and the people of the countryside, believed differently. For him, the rural culture he could see disappearing in his lifetime was just as important – if not more so – than any other in England because it represented what he believed was fundamental to a sustainable society.

As well as seeking a renewal of culture through a reconnection with local community and the land with a more harmonious marriage of tradition and modernity, Bell offers a further vision for the future of farming in England in *The Flower and the Wheel* in a chapter entitled 'Bread'. For him, bread is a 'symbol of yeoman independence, a reward of duties before rights […] a resurgent symbol'. It embodies the qualities that were being eroded through the changes in agricultural practices. Central to his vision of a more sympathetic and sustainable farming is the importance of good husbandry, as it is only through good husbandry that it is possible to provide local produce of quality:

Why should not government and people get together in a really imaginative idea for Britain? […] We have to only understand the nature of the material. Contemplate corn: respect the arts of husbandry. Hold to this central fact first – quality, the good quality of that peculiarly local product – food. Let us reintroduce good taste there first.

Although written over nearly seventy years ago, this passage would not look out of place in the introduction of numerous twenty-first century, organically minded chefs' glossy cookbooks. Bell knew that intensification – the dehumanizing of agriculture – might lead to cheaper food, but it would not lead to food of quality. In such an approach, understanding the 'nature of the material' is not a priority, whereas specialization for the purpose of mass production is. But Bell could see that this was not sustainable for either the farmer or the environment; the primary beneficiaries would be businesses away from either.

Consequently, in spite of (or because of) the technological advances of the last fifty years, England is arguably more divided – certainly economically – than it has ever been before. For companies such as Apple to have built up financial reserves that are larger than Singapore's is a clear indicator to the extent of the division's created by relentless capitalist consumerism. This rise in wealth and influence of such multinational companies comes at a cost to the individual, for he or she is encouraged to become a passive consumer, which is something that Bell could see happening increasingly during his lifetime. As he suggested himself in a different context, people are given the illusion of choice, but in reality most are manipulated by the persuasive marketing of national or incredibly powerful global companies.

This is opposite to the hope that Bell had for society, for two main reasons. Firstly, he believed that we should guard against embracing consumerism unquestioningly, as he saw that in doing so, power would be taken away from individuals. To become a consumer, you become reliant on others. Secondly, the influence of businesses whose interests were predominantly based in urban centres would most likely be negative to those living in rural England as their primary aim was to make money, and not to preserve the functioning of local communities. It is in this context that he made the following plea: 'Yet not forget to look further than to-day, and not forget the local life, and the peculiar quality of local earth, and the peculiar powers of local hands with the produce of local earth, which have been the shaping of us English, our constitutions and our characters.'

This 'local life' is of utmost importance because it is where knowledge, skills and a close relationship with the land can be found, and is where our characters are shaped. If we lose our sense of place, we are in danger of losing a sense of identity. The essayist and environmental activist Gary Snyder once wrote, quite wonderfully, 'Be famous for fifteen miles'. Bound up in this statement is a whole philosophy of life, and one that Bell lived his life by. Like John Clare, Bell's view may not have been broad, but it was deep. The land of which he writes is, primarily, a small part of his beloved Suffolk, and his deep connection with it is at the heart of his writing. This is why Bell was so passionate about the need to invest in rural communities in order to stem the tide of people moving away to the cities to find a living.

Moreover, Bell could not understand why it seemed acceptable to create a workforce that spent an inordinate amount of time undertaking bureaucratic tasks that mostly served urban business, when we were unable – or rather unwilling – to feed ourselves as a country. The idea that it is uneconomic to produce food is met with disdain by Bell, and is a notion that exemplifies how wrong he believes the priorities of policy makers are: 'Never yet has it been humanly uneconomic for a man to spend his day producing food, for never yet – not even in the history of this country – has there not been somebody with an aching void where his dinner should be.'

For him, living in a society that was encouraging the dismantling of rural communities in favour of serving the demands of capitalism would not only damage our identity – our character – as a nation, it would foster a more individualistic, selfish approach. Rather than live and work collaboratively, with an appreciation of co-dependency, working for companies would lead, for an increasing number of people, to a narrower view of their immediate world. Having a less holistic view of their interaction with others would also lead to a further disconnection between those who produce and those who consume. In turn, this would lead to a population who would become disconnected with their environment, viewing it as a commodity like any other – to be possessed and controlled so it may serve whatever needs we have.

Therefore, Bell's desire of a return to the land is not born out of nostalgia, it is a desire that encapsulates a number of things. It is a desire to create a society that values those who produce as well as those who consume. It is a desire that as many people as possible develop a connection with the land we live on, and what is done on it. It is a desire to re-establish a sense of place and a sense of harmony with our environment, and a sense of a shared purpose with each other.

To illustrate this vision, Bell quotes a passage from Laurence Stern, the eighteenth-century novelist. This passage, Bell notes, 'comes nearer than anything I could say to expressing that virtue in which men and women live and die happy.' In it, Stern depicts a family of three generations sitting down together for their evening meal of simple but locally produced food: 'I instantly borrowed that old man's knife, and taking up the loaf, cut myself a hearty luncheon; as I did it, I saw a hearty testimony in every eye, not only of an honest welcome, but of a welcome mixed with thanks'. For Bell, 'to live and die happy' you need a deep appreciation of all that sustains us: family, community and the land on which we depend. However, in a rapidly changing society this appreciation was in danger of being lost, and with it, a sense of what makes us who we are.

For Bell, farming and the values inherent in a sympathetic husbandry, symbolize a way of life that enables us to live and die happy. It is a way of life that connects us to the land, and to each other. This is why he makes clear his passion for farming throughout his writing, and why he believes that it should be valued more highly – and regarded more carefully – than it is. In doing so, he questions the movement from the land to specialized jobs that he views as restrictive to individuals and lacking in genuine purpose:

I now have care of this soil which former men have cherished. I feel such compulsion to it: it is the most important thing in life to me, far beyond the level of a paying proposition; because, I think, it is the greatest parable of ultimate truth, a sort of mystery play enacted year by year full in the face of people – factory operatives, politicians, technologists, industrial man-power, office personnel, and all other humans inhumanly labelled.

In contrast to his negative view of the plethora of new urban roles being created, he sees his role as a farmer very much in traditional terms: that is, a custodian of the countryside. Central to this role is the fundamental need to look after that on which all life on earth depends – soil. He feels such a 'compulsion to it' because he knows that if the soil is cared for, then it will provide not only for his generation, but also for generations to come. For him, this care for the soil, only achieved through a close and sympathetic relationship with it, is a 'parable of ultimate truth'. Without custodians who prioritize this relationship in their farming practices, there is a danger that we will destroy that on which we rely.

Bell lived through the second agricultural revolution during his lifetime. As the nature of husbandry changed beyond all recognition into industrial agriculture, he feared for the long-term consequences of the soil and the communities he so cherished. Although largely unheeded, Bell sounded a warning to farmers who were encouraged to buy into 'progressive' farming methods. In doing so, he sought to elevate the role of the farmer to 'a position of a prophet', particularly in the eyes of a growing urban population who were becoming more and more disconnected from the land.

'For all of Man's supposed accomplishments, his continued existence is completely dependent upon six inches of topsoil and the fact that it rains.' Bell's understanding of this fundamental truism, spoken by the Chinese philosopher Confucius 2,500 years ago, is central to his unwavering belief that farmers have a duty to – and responsibility for – the land they work – for the soil they till. It is a duty that should be as highly regarded by society as any other; there is nothing more important that producing food, and looking after the land on which this food is wholly dependent. Rather than being reduced to people who run a 'factory with the roof off', farmers should instead be flag bearers who remind us all of 'the primacy of man's daily bread' and the environment needed to produce it. They should offer a vision to all of society that we need to farm not only for the benefit of the people, but also for the long-term benefit of the land itself: it should be a vision of sustainability.

Thus Bell's respect for – and his connection with – the natural world lies at the heart of all his writing, from the opening pages of *Corduroy* to his final article in *The Eastern Daily Press*. He endeavours not to over-intellectualize this relationship, as he sees it as fundamental one in his life:

> I did not purposely set out to find a philosophy of living. I have merely sat, tired physically, when the day's work is done in the field, either in my arbour in summer, or before a fire in winter, and not consciously thought. Watched perhaps a swallow on a wire, with sunned breast up there when earth is all in shadow, or a bumblebee fastened on a saffron-headed helenium, black-and-gold heavy, swaying with the flower in a puff of wind. And some cell of me, tired with sowing turnips till the earth seemed to sway, knows the feeling of the bee clinging to the flower, swaying as it sways. The gulf of air beneath him, and the close warmth of yellow blazing into the many mirrors of his eyes. He had been bruised by the storm, and clung there against the sun-colour in a trance to survive.

An observer of nature cannot really understand what it is like to be truly linked to it unless they work closely with it: physical engagement is necessary for spiritual engagement. Although Bell did not seek a 'philosophy of living', it is clear that many years working as a farmer has led him to one. It is more than a deep appreciation of nature that he is portraying here, and in the majority of his writing: rather, it is a deep connection in which there is an inward correspondence to every outward living thing. Like the 'bee clinging to the flower, swaying as it sways', Bell understood, and articulated throughout his writing, that our life on this planet is dependent upon the natural world we are all part of.

EPILOGUE

So, WHAT HOPE IS there that the course on which farming in England has been on since *Corduroy* was first published can be changed? Can the smaller-scale, mixed farming for which Bell argues passionately throughout his writing meet the demands of a growing population, and to what extent is this achievable in our current society?

We live in one of the most fertile countries in the world, and have a population of over sixty-five million people. Despite this, we cannot sustain an agricultural economy in this country without subsidy. Food is a fundamental need, yet we relegate it in our economic priorities – cheaper is better. In England in 2018 we spent less than 8 per cent of our disposable income on food – this was over 30 per cent in the 1950s. When one considers the struggles farmers have had – and continue to have – with 'those vultures of the so-called open market', Bell's words are prescient. The power that the large supermarkets have on the farmers in Britain is well documented – they have maintained a stranglehold over agriculture in this country.

Currently, less than 20 per cent of the cost of our food goes to the farmers because of lengthy supply chains, with each link taking a cut, so the re-establishing of much stronger relationships between producers and consumers is fundamental if any shift in this ideology is to be achieved. But the blame for the lack of a healthy and sustainable agricultural economy should not be solely placed at the sliding doors of these huge businesses: we are all complicit. The vast majority of us, either through necessity or desire, want our food to cost as little as possible.

The recent expansion and popularity of budget supermarkets Lidl and

Aldi, and the price wars amongst the rest, is evidence of this. Consider any of their marketing, whether printed or moving image, and the main purpose of their rhetoric is to convey to us that if you shop with them you will get, to borrow a phrase, 'more for less'. Although they sometimes stress the quality of the food they sell, it is the bottom line – price – that dominates. So although supermarkets are hugely influential in changing the ideology and practices of farming in England, it ultimately comes down to consumer priorities.

Colin Tudge, a biologist and writer on science, agriculture and species diversity, attributes this indifference to the lack of a developed 'food culture' in England (unlike in countries such as France, Spain and Italy). In a chapter entitled 'The Absolute Importance of Food Culture' in his excellent book *Six Steps Back to the Land*, he emphasizes the point that we all have a responsibility to enact any change in the way we farm our countryside:

> Perhaps worst of all is that not enough of us give a damn. We don't put enough pressure on governments to take food and farming seriously. We allow ourselves to be conned into the belief that big-time farming and industrialization are necessary, and that they bring us cheaper food, which serious analysis shows is not the case. The British and Americans have developed a cheap food mentality: even those who can afford the best are inclined to opt for the cheapest, although these same people may have expensive cars and houses.

In order to give a damn, we must care about what food tastes like, how food is produced, and where it comes from. We need to educate ourselves about food, and not just pay lip service to it by watching endless cookery shows. Moreover, our attitude to food needs to be more like our attitude to other material goods, such as technology and cars – we must be prepared to pay for quality food. If we became responsible consumers of food, we could transform the destructive agriculture we currently have.

The American rural writer Wendel Berry believes it is crucial to reclaim elements of personal responsibility if any challenge to the status quo is to be effective. To illustrate this point, he argues that individuals must endeavour to become critical consumers rather than passive ones, focusing on their responsibilities, rather than their rights:

> If a consumer begins to think and act in consideration of his respon-
> sibilities, then he vastly increases his capacity as a person [...] A
> responsible consumer would be a critical consumer, would refuse to
> purchase the less good. And he would be a moderate consumer; he
> would know his needs and would not purchase what he did not need.

In addition to each of us taking more individual responsibility in what we choose to consume, there needs to be other changes if we are to move towards the type of traditional husbandry that Bell advocates in his writing. In *Six Steps Back to the Land*, Tudge outlines how farming could be directed towards Bell's vision. In doing so, he proposes that an agrarian renaissance is needed with 'enlightened agriculture' at its heart. He explains that enlightened agriculture has three main characteristics: firstly, agroecology, whereby farms need to be regarded as ecosystems. Secondly, food sovereignty, in which people should have more control over their food supply. Thirdly, both should be underpinned with eco-nomic democracy – this, having a moral dimension, prioritizes greater financial equality and advocates the formulation of mechanisms to benefit mankind and the biosphere. Because enlightened farms should be mixed, then by their very nature they need to be complex, and thus skills intensive. Therefore, such farms should be of small to medium size, and crucially, would require a return of labour to the land.

However, because land has become such a commodity, this makes any large-scale return to such small-scale farming problematic. The people with most power – corporates, banks, governments – continue to pursue high-input, industrialized agriculture, and argue that smaller scale, mixed farming is unable to produce the food that is needed to feed a growing population. This is true to a certain extent, but only because more sympathetic – and, as Bell highlighted in *The Green Bond*, more productive – methods of husbandry require people to work on the land:

Dear friends, arms and legs on small plots of this earth can produce vastly more than your soil-compressing giant tractors. Look at allotments: at country gardens. As the record yield of wheat this year was grown on a three-acre plot.

To achieve such levels of production from traditional methods of husbandry, Tudge suggests that at least 10 per cent of the working population in England should be involved directly with farming, and in some countries, up to 50 per cent. Currently, less than 2 per cent of the working population in Britain (and the US) work full-time in agriculture due to the industrialized nature of it. In India, this figure is 60 per cent.

He argues that 'In short, for most people in most countries, farming and all that goes with it is by far the best option. No other human pursuit could possibly supply all the jobs that humanity needs in a morally acceptable and sustainable fashion.' Therefore, if a move towards smaller-scale farming is to be achieved, then more people would need – and should be actively encouraged – to return to the land. For this to happen, the perception and status of farming would need to change. Rather than being viewed as something dominated by big machines or unskilled labourers, it should be regarded as a vocation, like teaching or medicine.

Consequently, there needs to be legal and financial mechanisms to support anyone who wishes to return to small-scale, mixed farming. Community farming is one way in which people have got involved in recent years – farming as joint endeavours can be practically and socially beneficial. Community-supported agricultures – known as CSAs – continue to grow both in the US and Britain. In addition, schemes such as Funding Enlightened Agriculture (FEA) and ethical investment companies and banks such as Gaeia, Ethex and Triodo, are enabling small farming enterprises to get off the ground. Furthermore, Tudge sees horticulture as the key to the agrarian renaissance, as 'it offers the principle route by which people at large can become involved in farming, so that enlightened agriculture and all that goes with it, ecologically, socially, and politically, can become the norm.'

There is hope that a return to an enlightened agriculture – or what

Bell calls traditional husbandry – is gathering momentum. For example, the importance – and the effectiveness – of small-scale, mixed farming was exemplified in a publication from the United Nations Commission on Trade and Development (UNCTAD) entitled 'Trade and Environment Review 2013: Wake Up Before It's Too Late'. The publication, which considers how agriculture must change in order to the feed a growing population in the context of climate change, included contributions from more than sixty experts from around the world. The report unequivocally advocates a move away from high chemical input, intensive agriculture, with two of its key recommendations being 'to drastically reduce the environmental impact of conventional agriculture [...] and broaden the scope for agro-ecological production methods.' This report reinforces the finding made by Professor Herren in the aforementioned *The World Agricultural Report* (2008) – that is, industrial agriculture is no longer fit for purpose if we are to feed our growing population and protect the six inches of topsoil that we are all dependent on.

In *Soil, Soul and Society: A New Trilogy for Our Time*, a book I urge everyone to read, Satish Kumar eloquently expresses the ideology that is integral to this vision of past, and perhaps future, husbandry. This is a vision that was – albeit in different terms –fundamentally shared by Bell:

> We need to shift from the old paradigm of fragmentation, dualism, disconnection, to a new paradigm of wholeness, connectedness and relatedness. This is a shift from big to small, global to local, machines and technology to human interaction and labour, hierarchy to networks and community, monoculture to cultural and biological diversity, control to participation.

If our current agricultural hegemony is to be effectively challenged and a more enlightened agriculture achieved, we cannot rely on others to do it for us. This shift must start with each of us recognizing that the farming we currently have is damaging our countryside, our farmers, our food, and us. It is only through this realization – this participation – that we will want, demand and deserve something better.

❧ BIBLIOGRAPHY ❧

Bell, Adrian, *Corduroy*, The Country Book Club, London, 1961 (1930)

Bell, Adrian, *Silver Ley*, Faber and Faber, London, 2008 (1931)

Bell, Adrian, *The Cherry Tree* (1932), Illustrated Edition, The Bodley Head, London, 1948

Bell, Adrian, *The Open Air*, Faber and Faber, London, 1936

Bell, Adrian, *Men and the Fields* (1939), Little Toller Books, Dorset, 2009

Bell, Adrian, *Apple Acre* (1942), Little Toller Books, Dorset, 2012

Bell, Adrian, *Sunrise to Sunset*, The Bodley Head, London, 1944

Bell, Adrian, 'The Small Farm' in *The Natural Order*, Massingham, H. J. (ed.), J. M. Dent, London, 1945

Bell, Adrian, *The Budding Morrow*, The Bodley Head, London, 1946

Bell, Adrian, 'Prince' in *Countryside Character*, Harman, Richard (ed.), Blandford Press, London, 1946

Bell, Adrian, 'Meeting a Man with a Horse-Rake' in *Countryside Mood*, Harman, Richard (ed.), Blandford Press, 1946

Bell, Adrian, *The Flower and the Wheel*, The Bodley Head, London, 1949

Bell, Adrian, *Music in the Morning*, The Bodley Head, London, 1954

Bell, Adrian, *A Suffolk Harvest*, The Bodley Head, London, 1956

Bell, Adrian, *My Own Master* (1961), The Country Book Club, London, 1962

Bell, Adrian, *A Countryman's Notebook*, The Boydell Press, Ipswich, 1975

Bell, Adrian, *The Green Bond*, The Boydell Press, Ipswich, 1976

Bell, Adrian, *A Countryman's Notebook*, Lucas Books, East Bergolt, 2001

Bell, Adrian, 'The Farm' in *England's Legacy* (1935), Batsford, London, 1961

Berry, Wendell, *The Unsettling of America: Culture and Agriculture* (1977), Counterpoint, Berkeley, 1996

Body, Richard, *Agriculture: The Triumph and the Shame* (1982), Temple Smith, London, 1983

Collis, John Stewart, *The Worm Forgives the Plough* (1946 & 1947; 1973), Vintage, London, 2009

Conford, Philip (ed.), *The Organic Tradition: An Anthology of Writings on Organic Farming 1900–1950*, Green Books, Devon, 1988

Earle of Portsmouth, *Alternative to Death: The Relationship Between Soil, Family and Community*, The Right Book Club, London, 1945

Easterbrook, L. F. (ed.), *Farming and Mechanised Agriculture*, Todd Publishing, London, 1945

Evans, Patrick, *A Hand to the Plough: A Farmer's Vision for the Twenty-first Century*, Sapey Press, Worcester, 2006

Gander, Ann, *Adrian Bell: Voice of the Countryside*, Holm Oak Publishing, Suffolk, 2001

Gardiner, C. H., *Your Village and Mine*, Faber and Faber, London, 1934

Harman, Richard (ed.), *Countryside Character*, Blandford Press, London, 1946

Harmon, Tony, *Seventy Summers*, BBC Publications, 1986

Harvey, Graham, *The Killing of the Countryside* (1997), Vintage, London, 1998

Harvey, Graham, *Grass-fed Nation: Getting Back the Food We Deserve*, Icon Books, London, 2016

Henderson, G., *The Farming Ladder*, Faber and Faber, London, 1934

Holderness, B.A., *British Agriculture Since 1945*, Manchester University Press, Manchester, 1985

Kingsnorth, Paul, *Real England: The Battle Against the Bland*, Portobello Books, London, 2008

Kingsnorth, Paul, *Confessions of a Recovering Environmentalist*, Faber and Faber, London, 2017

Kumar, Satish, *Soil, Soul, Society: A New Trilogy for Our Time*, Leaping Hare Press, Lewes, 2013

Lymbery, Philip with Oakeshott, I., *Farmageddon: The True Cost of Cheap Meat* (2014), Bloomsbury, London, 2015

Massingham, H. J., *The Wisdom of the Fields*, Collins, London, 1945

Massingham, H. J. (ed.), *The Natural Order: Essays in A Return to Husbandry*, J.M Dent, London, 1945

Massingham, H. J., *The Faith of the Fieldsman*, Museum Press Limited, London, 1951

Matless, David, *Landscape and Englishness* (1998), Reaktion Books, London, 2016

Monbiot, George, *Feral: Rewilding the Land, Sea and Human Life* (2013), Penguin, 2014

Pollen, Michael, *The Omnivore's Dilemma* (2006), Bloomsbury, London, 2011

Stapledon, George, *The Way of the Land*, Faber and Faber, London, 1943

Thomas, F. G., *The Changing Village*, Thomas Nelson, London, 1939

Tudge, Colin, *Six Steps Back to the Land*, Green Books, Cambridge, 2016

Williams, Raymond, *The Country and the City* (1973), Vintage, London, 2016

❧ INDEX ❧